Evil, Sexuality, and Disease

in

Grünewald's Body of Christ

Evil, Sexuality, and Disease
in
Grünewald's Body of Christ

Eugene Monick

WITH A FOREWORD BY DAVID L. MILLER

Spring Publications
Dallas

SPRING PUBLICATIONS, INC.
P.O. BOX 222069; DALLAS TX 75222
© 1993 by Spring Publications, Inc.
All rights reserved
Printed in the United States of America,
text on acidfree paper. First printing 1993

Cover designed and produced by Margot McLean
Cover image: detail of Christ from the Crucifixion panel of
Grünewald's Isenheim altarpiece
Reproduction of the cover image, as well as the fold-out color plates
of the altarpiece, © Musée d'Unterlinden, 68000 Colmar–France,
photograph by O. Zimmermann

Library of Congress Cataloging-in-Publication Data
Monick, Eugene, 1929–
Evil, sexuality, and disease in Grünewald's body of Christ /
Eugene Monick ; with a foreword by David L. Miller.
p.   cm.
Includes bibliographical references.
ISBN 0–88214–356–5 (pbk.)
1. Grünewald, Matthias, 16th cent. Isenheim Altar. 2. Grünewald,
Matthias, 16th cent.–Criticism and interpretation. 3. Jesus Christ
–Psychology. 4. Psychoanalysis and religion. 5. Good and evil.
6. Sex–Religious aspects–Christianity. 7. Body, Human–Religious
aspects–Christianity. 8. Health–Religious aspects–Christianity.
I. Title.
ND588.G7A645   1993
759.3–dc20   92–46068
                                                            CIP

And just as the conscious mind can put the question,
"Why is there this frightful conflict between good and evil?",
so the unconscious can reply,
"Look closer! Each needs the other. The best, just because
it is the best, holds the seed of evil,
and there is nothing so bad but good can come of it."

C. G. JUNG
TWO ESSAYS ON ANALYTICAL PSYCHOLOGY

Contents

ACKNOWLEDGMENTS		ix
FOREWORD BY DAVID L. MILLER		xi
	A Personal Introduction	1
1:	Fantasy as Hypothesis	10
2:	Grünewald: The Man and His Time	51
3:	Archetypes	75
4:	The Question of Disease in the Crucifixion Panel	89
5:	Christ and Evil	106
6:	Christ, Sexuality, and Disease	129
7:	Resurrection	170
	NOTES	178

Acknowledgments

I THANK THE MANY PEOPLE IN MY ZÜRICH YEARS WHO assisted me in this work, especially Helmut Barz, my thesis advisor. Also my wife, Barbara, my children, Stephen and Katherine. And Donald Poole, Alice Petersen, Jerry Donat, Odette Riemann, Carlo and Marie Abegg, Margaret Jacoby, David Roscoe, and, of course, long before Zürich, Albert Mollegen.

Since Zürich, I owe special gratitude to Dorcas Bankes, Alice Petersen again, James Hillman, David Miller, Greg Mogenson, Bessie Rohulich, Peter Grey, Percival Harris, and Mary Helen Sullivan.

In both times, I thank my analysands who provided a means of my testing psychic reality and who permitted my use of their material.

BLEMISHES WITHOUT BLEMISH

THIS WONDERFULLY READABLE WORK BY THE JUNGIAN ANALYST
Eugene Monick is about an equally wondrous, if difficult,
artwork. Grünewald's famous Isenheim altarpiece, now
located at Colmar in the Alsatian part of France, contains a
strange and troubling image: a portrayal of Jesus' body, skin
yellowed and greened, covered with pus and scabs, thoroughly
diseased. This image—what archetypal psychologists Rafael
Lopez-Pedraza, Niel Micklem, and Alfred Ziegler, following
the poet José Lesame Lima, have called an "intolerable
image"—constitutes both the wondrous and difficult dimensions of Monick's theme. Surprising as it may seem with so
distressing a topic, and like the Isenheim altarpiece itself, this
book offers relief, a "welcome remedy to incessant blame,"
as Monick himself puts it, an antidote to "the huge and
fruitless effort of seeking a perfect and stainless way." The
fascination, then, is in seeing how a blemished image of Jesus
paradoxically constitutes precisely a Christic sense of self
without blemish.

Facilitated by a therapeutic and properly pedagogical use
of real-life anecdotes, the reader will find in this book a story
that is psychologically intimate, yet never merely personal,
always concretely connected to particular human suffering,
but without being less archetypally important. Monick's work

is always homeopathic. Its healing power is, at least in part, in the way it handles Christianity psychologically.

In the psychological tradition following Jung, there have been two very different ways of treating religion in general and Christianity in particular. These two ways both have a basis in Jung.

On the one hand, the dominant view is that Jung was as soft on religion as Freud was hard on it, that Jung thought that the symbols and stories of religions are therapeutic and wholesome in function whereas Freud thought that the same religious materials are psychopathogenic, creating shame, guilt, and anxiety in the wake of childish dependencies and illusions. Indeed, Jung did argue that Christ is a symbol of selfhood, that the Roman Catholic Mass is a paradigm of the process of psychological maturation and individuation, that no psychoanalysis is finally complete until there has been a spiritual transformation, and that the archetypal images from the myths and religions of the world compensate the merely personal one-sidednesses of ego's everyday life. The Jungian writers who stress this side of Jung's perspective interpret religion by using psychological categories and thereby manage to rehabilitate religion's meanings positively. In this way, depth psychology becomes apologetic theology, saving Christianity for a postmodern world.

On the other hand, there are some Jungian writers who note that Jung's apparent psychological valorization of religion in general and Christianity in particular has another side. The Christ-image that Jung affirmed as a symbol of selfhood turns out to have been a gnostic-heretical Christ appealed to in the face of Jung's vehement criticism of Christianity's own orthodox understanding. The Mass that Jung draws upon as symbolic of psychological development is a ritual reinterpreted by way of the barbarous pagan rites of the Aztecs. Furthermore, Jung blamed low self-esteem on the Christian theological doctrine concerning evil (*privatio boni*), saying that people suffer Christianity in their psychological feelings as much as they suffer from problems of personal history. And concerning what one might call unconscious theological abuse, Jung referred to Christianity as "a big monster, a great snake" that he as a physician was attempting to "wrestle." The Jungian writers who stress this side of Jung's perspective see the shades and shadows of Christianity and interpret human psychological suffering with a hermeneutic of religious images, viewing religion as a part of the symptomatic problem of the individual and collective psyche in our time. In this way, depth psychology becomes a new "theology," saving people from the unconscious ravages of a former religiosity that was one-sided.

If the author of this book began his work with Grünewald in 1977 on the positive psychological side of the religion, he has in 1992 ended it on the shadow side. This book places him in the company of analysts such as John Dourley, Adolf Guggenbühl-Craig, Greg Mogenson, Charles Asher, Wolfgang Giegerich, and James Hillman, that is, those who look to religion for the etiology of the "illnesses that we are." It also implicates the author homeopathically.

The psychological interpreters of religion who value Christianity's images for their positive healing power typically, if unwittingly, commit themselves to an allopathic perspective. *Allos* in Greek means "other." Allopathic medicine attempts to heal by supplying what is lacking or demanded, like giving Geritol for iron-poor blood. On this view, religion provides what ego lacks—faith, hope, love, spirit, grace, and all the rest of the ascensional virtues and feelings.

But there may at times be a problem with an allopathic perspective in the face of psychological suffering. When, for example, a person is in the midst of grief, he or she does not want some well-intended allopathic healer to say, "Oh, cheer up! Things are going to be all right." This is not only unhealing, but it is also unfeeling. The same is true in the case of depression or low self-esteem. In these situations what may be most needed therapeutically is an image for expressing the grief, the depression, or the worthlessness and emptiness. To give image to the shade or shadow would be homeopathic, healing "like with like" (*similia similibus curantur*). On this view, religion can help by being a vessel for tortured, twisted sufferings—but only if its images are as "intolerable" as the feeling of the individual who is hurting. We gain access to our sufferings through religion's negative images; and we get leverage on the shadows of, say, Christianity through the likenesses of our own wounds. Grünewald's dis-eased Christ is "without blemish" because it, with simple purity, is just like our blemishes.

To be sure, this is not pretty. It acknowledges with Jung, sometimes painfully, that oppositions belong together, at least in the synchrony of the psyche (*complexio oppositorum*), and this is not an easy insight to live with. Indeed, the authentic homeopathic potency of this book did not come easily to its author, himself originally trained as an Episcopal priest. But, if the work has grown between 1977 and the present moment into something less Christian and less Jungian, at least in the doctrinal and orthodox senses of these two traditions, it may nonetheless, and precisely by reason of this growth, be now more deeply "Christian" and more profoundly "Jungian" than one might have been able at first to imagine. By transforming the letter of a religion and a psychology into their abysmal spirit, the author courageously allows the reader to retrace the journey of his homeopathic discovery, the discovery which reveals that blemishes experienced thoroughly may serve to release the soul from its sense of inherited blemish. As T. S. Eliot put it:

> The wounded surgeon plies the steel
> That questions the distempered part;
> Beneath his bleeding hand we feel,
> The sharp compassion of the healer's art
> Resolving the enigma of the fever chart.
> Our only health is the disease
> If we obey the dying nurse
> Whose constant care is not to please
> But to remind of our, and Adam's curse
> And that, to be restored,
> Our sickness must grow worse.

The present book is an artful and moving testimony to the psychological truth of Eliot's poetic insight.

DAVID L. MILLER

WATSON-LEDDEN PROFESSOR OF RELIGIONS

SYRACUSE UNIVERSITY

A PERSONAL INTRODUCTION

THIS WORK BEGAN AS MY DIPLOMA THESIS, WRITTEN IN 1977 for the C. G. Jung Institute, Zürich. It was a Jungian project by a Christian priest, a somewhat tentative exploration of an explosive correlation of sensuality, psychology, and religion. Grünewald's Isenheim Crucifixion was the medium for the correlation; body, psyche, and faith were drawn together within Grünewald's disturbing figures. Over the years since 1977, the painting has been a catalyst for, a container of, my theological/psychological/erotic imagination. The work, both Grünewald and what I have made of it, has evolved into something which is neither Christian nor Jungian, strictly speaking. It is now more gnostic, more personal, more strangely incongruous with my background, certainly as an ordained person but now also as a therapist.

To me, Jung's most radical moral idea was his insistence that evil pervades reality, up to and including our human knowledge of God. That notion, applied to the Grünewald and to my emotional experience with it, stands behind everything that is written in these pages.

Christianity came first. I was raised in St. Paul in a family with no church affiliation, a rarity in the 1930s and 40s in a nice middle-class, middle-western family. Though the family was not religious, it was moral almost to a fault, as though a tiny false move, even a false word, might bring down the house. The only cultic practice was Masonic, and that was secret, obscure, off to the side. My father's out-front belief was in America and the Republican Party. My mother went along.

Since the other children in the neighborhood were going to Sunday School, I asked my parents to send me. Everyone around us was Lutheran, or a pietistic derivation thereof. On the East Side of St. Paul at that time, the domicile of some seventy-five thousand people, there was one each Methodist, Presbyterian, Congregational, Episcopal, and Roman Catholic congregation, all small and struggling. The Lutherans and their offshoots had some thirty churches, including several that were very large. My father had something of a Presbyterian background, so my brother, sister, and I went to the Arlington Hills Presbyterian Church. It was an unlikely place, full of gospel hymns and crepe-paper hallelujas. Later, in my teen-aged years, I discovered the Episcopal Church for myself, downtown, where formality and the suggestion of mystery were a surprising and welcome relief. A catholicism that was not Roman Catholicism was the first of my conversions.

My interest in Grünewald began when I was a student at the Episcopal Theological Seminary in Alexandria, Virginia in the early 1950s. I learned of the Isenheim altarpiece from my professor of moral theology, Albert Mollegen. He spoke of it only once as I recall, but that once was formidable. I remember his describing it as the greatest Christian expression of God's suffering and Grünewald as the most courageous Christian who had ever painted.

His explanation was more revolutionary than anything I'd ever heard about Jesus, so much so that it became a kind

2

of sub-text to my understanding of Christianity, an off-set to my closely guarded high-church sanctity. Mollegen said that Grünewald painted Jesus in the Crucifixion panel of the Isenheim altarpiece as having syphilis, the scourge of human sexuality. I was dumbstruck. A sexual Jesus? The thought had never seriously entered my mind. A Jesus dead from his love certainly had, but his being dead from his sexual love was exhilaratingly iconoclastic; it cut a wide swath through both convention and inhibition. And this from a foremost Church apologist! I was fascinated and deeply moved by Mollegen's imagination, but I found no way to put such an idea into the context of my new priesthood. It simmered for years beneath my orthodoxy.

Twenty-five years later, as I wrote on Grünewald in Zürich, Mollegen reacted in shock at my suggestion that he had said such a thing: "You seem to be all mixed up."[1] I can suppose that, with age, a degree of Mollegen's radicality had diminished. Be that as it may, for me the image of a Christ so demeaned has stuck. It served as a subliminal counterpoint, through my years of ministry prior to my Zürich training, to my tendency toward a theological triumphalism exalting Christ to a position far removed from worldly weakness and limitation. It was ironic, albeit appropriate to the Isenheim, that the man who first suggested this astonishing interpretation refused corroboration at the time of my conscious development of his image. Mollegen's refusal was right in a way. But as I see it, my "mix-up" has been the starting point of imaginal wanderings that have led me out and beyond old places that needed to be left behind.

From 1954 to 1975, I practiced the ministry of the Episcopal Church in Michigan, Minnesota, and New York. In 1959 I

3

became an executive for the Episcopal Church in college and university work in New York and shared an office with William Kennedy, then head of the Episcopal Council for Foreign Students which he founded. We became friends. He introduced me to Jung's work. In 1965, I was appointed vicar of an experimental theater-church, St. Clement's, near Times Square in Manhattan. At the same time, my Jungian analysis began, bringing an emerging understanding of the archetypal basis of myth and ritual which enriched and gave meaning to the liturgical innovations of ten remarkable years at St. Clement's.

Sensuality, archetypal psychology, and Isenheimian Christianity were coming into contact. The image of a Christ infused with eroticism coalesced in the week-by-week presence of the sacrament, broken in my hands, in a congregation alive with sexual revolution. A time came when I could no longer withstand the onslaught of war resistance, theater, weekly liturgical creations, feminism, and New York's incessant blotting of energy. In 1972, with my wife and our two children, I went to Zürich on a year's sabbatical leave.

Midway, friends who savored expensive French restaurants suggested that we join them at the Auberge de L'Ill outside of Colmar, in Alsace on the German–French border. While we are there, they said, we might also see the Grünewald Isenheim altarpiece. It was my initiation rite into the second half of life.

On a Saturday evening in February of 1973, the four of us gorged ourselves on the world's best food and drink, the world's best friendship, in the world's most luxurious restaurant. It was a feast of instinct, an epitome on one side of the scale of human experience, archetypal in its own right.

On Sunday morning, before the Grünewald Crucifixion, Barbara and I wept, like simple fools. We entered the Unterlinden museum, looked, walked past the other panels of the altarpiece, came again before the Crucifixion, and sat on the bench set before it almost as a pew, stunned. I remember that she, the stoic, allowed it to come first. I remember noticing her tears with amazement, recalling how proud she was at not being a believer.

A friend once wrote of his wife and children in Washington in 1969, walking, from their chartered bus after riding all night, toward the White House with three hundred thousand others in a demonstration against the Vietnam War, and likening it to "a living rosary." So were Barbara's tears for me. But with a difference, all important. In those public years when we did those Washington things, we hoped that everyone would notice, that the world would be different because of our action. In Colmar on that Sunday in 1973, Barbara and I were all but oblivious to what must have been the spectacle we made of ourselves sitting on that bench, weeping. It was an intensely private, inner experience.

That moment of Barbara's and my connection to one another through the Grünewald Crucifixion is a demonstration to me of the presence of an archetypal image. I know something has happened because I experience it, I feel it, my emotions tell me. The tears well up; they pay no mind to the public place. Ordinary reserve is no longer a restraint. "Archetypal image," as word, as print, leaves a sterile, academic impression. Yet the moment, for me, was a vortex of recapitulation—of Mollegen's awesome lecture at Virginia Seminary; of the years of ambition, trial-and-error, fear, and accomplishment at St. Clement's; of the futility of opposi-

tion to a homeland swirling toward self-destruction; of pushing the ego as far as it would go in marriage, parenthood,
friendship, and love. The muddiness of my mid-life confu-
sions, of my personal fears, of my yearning for resolution was
present in a flash of water on the cheek. An end was
prefigured. I was given a sign that a serious and determined
effort to "turn it around," as we said in the sixties, by my
own conscious effort was drawing to a close. Barbara and I
sat as two innocents, crying, as the tourists came and went,
before the crucified and desperately ill Jesus, dying because
of his love.

After the sabbatical year we returned to New York in 1973
and in 1975 returned to Zürich to finish the diploma. Barbara and I went once more to Colmar. This time there were
no outpourings. We saw, we remembered, we went away to
discuss how the threads that jumped together before the
Grünewald might be woven into a dissertation. There was
not the same shock–that happened only on the first encounter. But there continued–and continues–to be the
presence of mystery. The numen, the spirit of the piece,
remains.

In 1977, after the thesis, I began a practice of Jungian
psychoanalysis in New York City and Scranton, Pennsylvania.
In 1989, I went back to Zürich on another sabbatical to re-
work the thesis for publication. I was drawn back to it. The
Isenheim had a life within me that had not yet come to
completion.

The curious power of the Isenheim seems to be growing, the more so, I believe, as conventional Christianity fades
in its ability to touch the depths of the unconscious in an
increasingly numbed and exhausted Western society. More-

6

over, as syphilis has faded away as an illness, AIDS has appeared as a world contamination, largely spread by sexual contact. AIDS, as such, was unknown in 1977, as syphilis was unknown by that name at the time of Grünewald's painting of the Isenheim Crucifixion.

Still another reason for my writing is my present age. When I first heard Mollegen speak of Grünewald I was twenty-three years old, freshly into a seminary and a vocation that I entered innocently, ignorant of the complexity and profundity of human sexuality, especially my own. When I first saw the Isenheim with Barbara, I was forty-four years old and deeply enmeshed in my struggle with something old passing away and something new coming into focus. My later sabbatical in Zürich celebrated sixty years, another rite of passage, into age. The Isenheim has been associated with my times of "crossing over," of moving from one stage of my life to another.

In preparation for my 1989 sabbatical, I read Anthony Storr's *Solitude*. He speaks of the third, or late, period of life as "a time when communication with others tends to be replaced by works depending more upon solitary meditation" and quotes Bernard Berenson defining genius (I would say, creativity) as "the capacity for productive reaction against one's training."[2]

As I write this now, forty of my sixty-two years have had Grünewald's Crucifixion as an abiding, if subliminal, and quietly burning image. The seeds which have matured into this work were preceded by two adult twenty-year stages, as Storr suggests. In my first, I relied upon the church's voice. In my second, an individuality began to take hold. As my last stage begins, it is time to share my fantasy. It is necessarily subjective, and it is clear to me now, as never before, that general truth is always found in the personal experience of one's own truth, which is simultaneously psychological and religious.

It is personal in the physicist Michael Polanyi's sense, that "acts of comprehension are to [an] extent irreversible, and also non-critical. . . . Such is the *personal participation* in all acts of understanding."[3] It is subjective and psychological in Jung's sense, viz.: ". . . the subjective factor [is] . . . that psychological action or reaction which merges with the effect produced by the object and so gives rise to a new psychic datum."[4] It is gnostically religious in Stephan Hoeller's sense that "the ideas which form the content of every religion are not primarily the product of an externally originating revelation, but of a subjective revelation from within the human psyche."[5]

Polanyi also says, "such knowing is indeed *objective* in the sense of establishing contact with a hidden reality. . . . It seems reasonable to describe this fusion of the personal and the objective as Personal Knowledge."[6] I tell my fantasy with bits and pieces of my own story, homely and commonplace as they are, seeming to fall randomly into place as they occur, which is how archetypal presences are known to ordinary people. Precisely because they are personal, and subjective, their inclusion authenticates the objective nature of Grünewald's vision in a psychological sense and qualifies my vision as religious. The gospel writers told their story of Jesus; Grünewald painted his story of the Crucifixion; and I write of my story with Grünewald. I make no claim for its validity as everyone's truth, any more than did Grünewald or, I'd like to think, say, St. Luke. In Polanyi's words, the question for each of us is whether or not there is "contact with a hidden reality."

It may be time for my story to be more than a solitary meditation.

I

FANTASY AS HYPOTHESIS

I INVITE THE READER TO ACCOMPANY ME ON A FANTASY.
Jung stands out amongst the founders of depth psychology in his respect for fantasy. He allowed fantasy to illuminate his understanding of the unconscious. He wrote that ". . . what, with us, is a subterranean fantasy was once open to the light of day."[1] Without his influence, my early amazement at Mollegen's suggestion might have remained an undeveloped flash of possibility, too far-fetched for anything but wonder, closed in the dead of night.

I am indebted as well to the work and person of James Hillman, Jung's most original modern exponent. His unflinching advocacy of fantasy has urged my confidence in invention; without it, my wonder at the Isenheim Crucifixion might lie buried still beneath a pall of convention. Hillman believes fantasy to be the *lingua franca* of imagination and imagination the *lingua franca* of psyche. Fantasy seen this way is considerably more than the defensive escape from reality to which Freud objected. Fantasy, however derided by common sense, imprisoned by literalness, is the raw material of human possibility reaching into consciousness. So understood, even ordinary imagination is a means by which human beings find themselves touching transcendence. Fantasy is brushed with the sacred, whether found in great art, in the soul of the observer of the art, or in the soul of the person with no apparent connection whatsoever with art or greatness.

Our error, often, is to consider transcendent human experience as something extraordinary, something rare and of major consequence. Ordinary stuff is thus cut off, preventing everyday discovery of meaning found in the commonplace, an interaction of banality and what pops open one's eyes as implication, the more-than-what-is-obvious. Yet fantasy is quite obvious, coming upon us every time we slip into undirected reflection, every time something occurs to us when we're not looking. Banal transcendence is that step into meaning occurring to us in chance thought, in the peripheral notion that flies away dismissed as absurdity. That we usually pay no serious attention to our fantasy but pay enormous amounts of money to see and read and listen to someone else's is a sign of our being out of touch with our own sacredness, our inner source.

A fantasy, as an experienced event of common transcendence, enters our mind and organizes our thinking at some specific point, a point I have chosen to call, for the purposes of this chapter, "hypothesis."

My friend Peter Grey was with me for a week in Zürich in 1989 at the beginning of my re-writing. He saw this chapter, then called "Fantasy and Concept." He vigorously disapproved of "concept": "It is too Germanic and too intellectual." "Just what I want," I shot back. I had hoped to compensate for the ephemeral quality of fantasy, for my insecurity in writing imaginatively. I wanted a reader to weave in and out with me through fancy and idea, to grasp the psychological quality of my view of the Isenheim. I was leaning heavily on "concept" as a shield against flimsiness. "Concept" had a tough quality about it. Peter insisted upon "hypothesis." "Hypothesis" sounded more flexible, more tentative. If I were to think soft maybe I'd write hard.

The point of this chapter is to set a stage for what is to come. I have experienced moments in theater when I have intuitively grasped the entire concept of the author and director through an environment created by the designer. I have been in my seat when the curtain rose to reveal the setting and joined the audience in spontaneous applause before a movement was made on stage.

To some of my readers, Grünewald's Isenheim Crucifixion may be well-known. If so, an attitude about the work has already been formed; a jolt is needed to open space for the juice of fantasy to flow, as that happened to me when I heard Mollegen's lecture on Grünewald. I did not know Grünewald, but of course I knew the crucifixion. I was in seminary because of the crucifixion. I was a devotee of the crucifixion, having moved from Protestant pietism to Anglo-Catholic sacramentalism only shortly before. Then came the shock, from a professor with authority, that Grünewald depicted the crucified Christ as suffering a venereal disease. My astonishment became a dawning of new consciousness.

This work is the evolution of that dawning of consciousness. It is not a work of art history or criticism or aesthetics, for which I have no professional competence. It is enough that a reader might say a tentative "aha," or "I see what he means," or "maybe." Fantasy proves nothing; it suggests. Within the confines of one reality it insinuates another. Fantasy is the antithesis of scholarship. But even scholars have approached the Isenheim with an interpretational latitude as in, for example, Andrée Hayum's observation that ". . . this altarpiece calls up a wider perspective accessible to anthropological scrutiny."[2]

Aporia might be an apt description for the way I intend to proceed. Aporia is "a systematic reflection upon a paradox so that one is slowly led through its complexities," according to Robinson Lillienthal.[3] Aporia, a Greek word, means doubt. Complexity surely abounds both in the Isenheim Crucifixion and in the interior world of the observer. Doubt arises from an inadequacy in explanations of the complexity; from the doubt comes the urgency for "systematic reflection," a process that appears to be rational but which might just as well be fantastic, if imagination rather than logic were the means to untangling the complexity. If so, fantasy can be a means of playing with doubt, and the process can be the way of aporia.

Another way of my describing my working with Grünewald might be anagoge, a Greek word meaning "to lead up" or, better, "away from" a literal or concrete interpretation, toward a mystical, meta-physical frame of reference. Jung credits Silberer as first discovering "the secret threads that lead from alchemy to the psychology of the unconscious"[4] and connects Silberer's interest in the anagogic significance, say, of a dream with his own synthetic or progressive (as opposed to Freud's reductive) approach to the psyche.[5] Unless one is led away from literalism, one is imprisoned in the ego, caught in the prosaic. Vision is gone.

I will work with my fantasy as a hypothesis and invite the reader to accompany me on an exploration. Fantasies can be read or worked with "as if" they were hypotheses, which, of course, they are, long before a hypothesis is conceptualized. One might say that fantasy is to the psyche as hypothesis is to the physical world. Fantasy is an invitation to embark upon a psychological exercise in imagination.

Three thoughts on fantasy and hypothesis:

1. The argument between Peter and me about the title of this chapter is, in itself, a fantasy, a different way to connect one's mental dots. The switch from "concept" to "hypothesis" was a move from a Latin- to a Greek-rooted word for the same intention. "Concept" has a more feminine etymological basis, from the Latin *concipere*, to conceive, an organic and sexual activity. "Concept," linguistically, coincides with "fantasy" within a feminine frame of reference. Men today, unless they are artists, usually find it difficult—even embarrassing—to openly take pleasure in fantasy. It is somehow beneath them, as it was beneath Freud. The masculine is likely to think and do. It does not easily allow, even less follow, fancy.

"Hypothesis" has linguistically a ring of the masculine about it. *Hypo*, in Greek, denotes that which is under, and *tithenai* means to put. Hypothesis, then, means that which is put under, viz., a foundation. Such a notion is structural in implication.

Interestingly, my friend Peter, wanting less intellectuality, suggested a word etymologically more structural, more phallic, more logos in tone, though its connotation seemed to both of us more "feminine." This little story in itself demonstrates the importance of fantasy. Associations in one's mind when a cross and a dead figure are seen may be quite conventional. Fantasy opens one to strange and heretofore unimagined connections.

2. Everyday experience provides evidence of archetypal

presence in human life. Fantasy is story imagined from experience, however banal.

During my sabbatical, I was in a department store in Zürich looking for stationery supplies. A saleslady was putting the contents of cartons of envelopes, paper, pens, etc., on shelves. Eyes glaring, she was a compulsive in her ripping open of the warehouse boxes, bustling through the aisles, and stacking the proper bins. In a way, she was typically Swiss, multiplied by ten. She caught my eye and I could not look away, so frenetic and single-minded was her performance. On one of her trips, she plowed into a woman casually examining something on the opposite side of the aisle. The customer stood dumbfounded, nearly spun-around by the force of the encounter. A tornado had hit her, without so much as an acknowledgment.

The saleslady was going about her appointed task. If someone got in her way, it was unfortunate for that someone. The customer stood for a moment, staring into space, adjusting herself to the affront. Then she turned around in the aisle behind the putting-things-where-they-belong saleswoman, pulled her arms across her chest, slammed into the compulsive clerk, and walked out of the store. The clerk's rage could be heard several departments away. Her arms flew into the air. Schweitzer-Deutsche epithets flew from her mouth. Had the cashier seen that? People are crazy these days! You can't even do your job! Every customer in that part of the store stared in astonishment.

Fantasy everywhere. Fantasy in the clerk . . . in the customer . . . in the cashier (who laughed and laughed and who, I suspect, had been waiting for just such an event) . . . and in me. As I write this, I am aware that I was caught in a fantastic world at that moment, and I am now as the scene turns in memory and I connect it to, of all things, Grünewald.

The homely story of the department store lady works in the same way as Barbara's and my sitting before the Crucifixion: an eruption of only-barely-mediated emotion overwhelms the ego. What came pouring from me as I saw her tears? How can I know unless I weave the loose threads of the fantasy together?

Fantasy produces mood and the emotions of mood, even as mood produces fantasy. Raw nerve is exposed in screaming at the top of one's lungs about a rude customer and in standing glued to the silly scene taking place before one's eyes. Shopclerk? I do the same thing. I have been as besotted by task and self-righteous as the clerk, as mindlessly careened into as the customer. I've had enough and I've paid back. Even now I do it. I sit at my screen playing with words to convey a wrenching moment—Barbara's eyes in Colmar, my eyes seeing her eyes, reflecting to me a gathering of memories swirling around passion, divinity, darkness, fear, and the shred of balance upon which my life was and is hung. Is such a thing religious, or the antithesis of religion, as in decadence, utility, despair? I see in it god upon a cross—sick, pustuled, as the men in the Isenheim hospice—crippled, stuck in a social crevasse as was the department store clerk—as helpless as anyone is helpless when enmeshed in a wellspring of adversity. I have spoken in two churches about the Isenheim. In one where I had preached often, I was never asked to do so again. In the other, I was told that two families left the congregation after my presentation. The woman who invited me was astounded by this reaction. She assumed that an imaginative work on a crucifixion would be interesting to church members, even if it were esoteric.

Not necessarily. Clearly there are limits. And one prevailing limit, so it seems, is that Jesus does not share the lot of actual humanity. In creeds we can say that he does, but one must be quite careful about applying creedal orthodoxy to ordinary life.

3. There is no psychoanalysis without storytelling. The stories become interesting once they are liberated from the oppression of moralism, literalism, and dogma, once imagination is free to range. One person tells a story; the other responds with a story, ordinarily called an intervention. Even when nothing is said in a session, story is told.

The ebb and flow of story is a product of fantasy. It may be that a good analyst is one who has a wide range of stories at his/her disposal, a subtle ability to connect, and a refined sense and practiced knowledge of when and how to tell and not to tell. The same is true of religion, whose core is the telling of ancient story. Places of worship "speak" without a word, even when specific images are sparse. Swiss Reformed churches, cleared of pictures at the Reformation, tell their own cleansed story. The sense of presence in a holy place is like the authority of story supercharged with meaning/fantasy in an individual life, even when there is hardly anything there.

When re-writing this work in Switzerland in 1989, I heard a BBC announcer tell a story about Noel Coward, in a West End comedy at the time, speaking with an actress playing the part of the Virgin in *Miracles*, another West End play. She said to Coward, "I saw your play the other night. Never once did I laugh." He turned to her and replied, "I saw yours and I roared with laughter." To appreciate that choice bit of classy British wit, one must know something of Holy Scripture as well as the nature of theater-talk, with its narcissistic tone. It also helps to know a bit about Coward's capacity for arch contempt, particularly of women he could not tolerate. Associations pour in. An American from the Middle West, hearing an English story in Europe, can chuckle for an hour at a remark so quintessentially imperious that a note on the whole of a man's life is struck. And a note on human vainglory, class, and bitterness as well – all of which go far beyond Coward's life, beyond the British, beyond theater.

As an analyst listens to story, a pattern forms in his or her mind and an idea is conceived. Not a new idea, perhaps, but one newly connected to the storyteller. A story-as-response-to-this-story, a hypothesis – in my words, a fantasy – begins to emerge. Robertson Davies puts these words into the mouth of Dr. van Haller in his novel *The Manticore*.

We have agreed, have we not, that everything that makes a man great, as opposed to merely a sentient creature, is fanciful when tested by what people call common sense? That common sense often means no more than yesterday's opinions? That every great advance began in the realm of the fanciful? That fantasy is the mother not only of art, but of science as well?[6]

Story, as fantasy, thus becomes the basis for concept – for conception, if one is to take a feminine direction; for hypothesis, if the direction is masculine. The mixture is one of artifice and empirical reality, where an awareness of, say, "human vainglory, class, and bitterness" begins to take shape and an attitude about the combination crystallizes. Forms, patterns, shapes, common images are the way we speak about what Jung called archetypes, the hypothetical, inherited, instinct-like foundation elements of psyche. Archetypes are repeated in endless imagistic variations, in as many variations, presumably, as there are stories.

A work of art, Grünewald's Isenheim Crucifixion in this case, is as much story as is the clever Noel Coward snippet or the Swiss department store scene. It is a more important story, so we think, because of Grünewald's skill and imagination and because of the traditional and valued subject matter. Yet a radical element in Jung's view of the archetype is the commonality, the inevitability, of archetypal patterns in all of life, trivial as well as monumental. Human uniqueness has to do with personal breakthroughs in the discovery of patterns and their variations—noteworthy genius, where one person's creativity is useful to others, and everyday genius, where one enjoys disclosure in solitude.

In the observing as well as in the making of art, the pattern—archetype—emerges, obliquely referent to "yesterday's opinions." Someone writing about a work of art should know something, of course, about "yesterday's opinions": the history of the piece and its criticism. What is not so well understood is the necessity of individual variations and their validity—what I am calling fantasy—in interpretation. Without it, nothing new happens, or nothing inches toward newness. We repeat, we see and hear in the form that we have seen and heard before. There is no emotion poulticed from beneath the surface because everything is familiar.

Now let me introduce my hypothesizing about Grünewald's painting, distillations from my numinous experience with it and from my puzzling about the relationship between sexuality and the sacred and about the nature of divinity that it portrays.

THE DARK CHRIST

My impression of Christ, in general, encompasses the range of experiences I have known in my own life raised to their highest power. By extension, the Christ figure includes within itself the experience of humankind, far beyond the limitations of what I know personally. Further, Grünewald's Isenheim Crucifixion tells me that nothing known to the human race is unknown to the Christ figure painted on the altarpiece cross.

My emphasis regarding the Isenheim Crucifixion is malady, "the illness that we are," as John Dourley has said.[7] Grünewald has painted a diseased Christ. The scriptural account has Jesus taken by Roman soldiers, beaten, hung upon a tree to die of torture and exposure. However, as I see Grünewald's painting, an interior affliction was primary and lethal; the outer assault was but apparently instrumental in his death. The confounding message of Grünewald's Crucifixion is that an inner process of disintegration has taken place. His outer wounds are ostensible. The painting conforms to scripture. But something more is implied.

According to orthodox Christian tradition, this "something more" is an absurdity. Jesus as Christ is presented as without inherent blemish. Jesus' crucifixion is understood as the result of sinful humanity's inability to live in the presence of perfection. Christ suffered precisely because he is blameless; humankind is ontologically guilty, before, during, and after the cross. The crucified Christ bountifully took – and takes, since the historical sacrifice upon the cross was a cosmic action – upon himself the sin of humanity, paying the price that humanity cannot pay, since all of it is tainted with original sin and therefore no human offering is worthy. Only the Lamb of God is innocent. Humankind is saved through faith in the efficacy of the mighty act of God's mercy shown on the cross. Christ's pain is the result of what was done *to* him, certainly not because of any intrinsic taint in himself.

It is not my intention to dispute orthodox Christian tradition. But tradition is not the only way to understand God. Certainly it is not the way to inner knowing. Experience is.

If one reads Grünewald's Christ from a psychological-phantasmagorical viewpoint, as a product of a feverish imagination, one enters a world closer to the patients of Isenheim. Fever, heating up of the body in response to illness and, also, metaphorically, desire, raises the temperature of fancy as well. Fancy as fever, as in the archetypal fantasy, say, of the torch song, is the attitude of passionate love. Passionate love is close to my imagination about Grünewald, following Mollegen, and it strikes me as appropriate to mention torch songs, which, if my argument holds, can express archetypal reality as much as does my fantasy, or Mollegen's, or Grünewald's, or Jung's or Hillman's, for that matter. As the reader will note further on, even scholars respected for their painstaking research on Grünewald are drawn into observations of wildness and heat regarding the Isenheim. Fever, one might guess, was omnipresent among the patients at

Isenheim; certainly it is a constant thread in the lives of all sick persons, lovers, and mystics. It is dangerous and it is dark.

DARK CHRIST: EVIL

A radical and disturbing ingredient of Jung's speculations was his insistence that good and evil are inextricably co-present in the psyche. I understand this to mean that there can be no good without co-present evil, no evil without good standing at the threshold waiting to be enjoyed. Within the limited capacity of the ego, it is extraordinarily difficult to find even a thread of good in much that appears to be evil; more apparent is a rumbling of evil beneath the surface of good. Jung's insistence upon evil is thus difficult to comprehend, particularly when one is in the throes of a much-desired experience. So pervasive is the notion in the Western world that evil is not intrinsic to life that it is almost always seen as intrusive, essentially alien, and "someone's" responsibility.

Even more difficult is an actual integration of evil as a valid part of one's understanding of daily, matter-of-fact existence. Ordinarily, we expect goodness and we gasp at evil. Evil is a usurper, a foreigner, a stranger in our midst, against which we lock our doors, hire our guards, build our hospitals. We go to great lengths to ignore evil and then, when it cannot be ignored, to confine and destroy it, all with unquestioned public approval.

Jung's thinking on the dark side of life was rooted in the complex stories he encountered in himself and his patients. He included evil in his rather quaint designation – shadow – which should fool no one into thinking the less of it. Each human being has a shadowy, dark side to his/her personality, which the ego seeks to hide, necessarily, up to a point, if it is to have the strength it needs to survive. In adult psychoanalysis, however, one must seriously encounter one's darkness and begin the process of including it in one's personal definition. To ignore or to try to root out evil is a childish illusion, therapeutically, bringing on subtly debilitating psychological consequences.

Jung's pungent awareness of darkness in an individual took him far beyond the vicissitudes of individual misfortune. Shadow is archetypal, ontological, and substantial, and as unavoidable an opposite to light as night is to day. Social evil and cosmic evil exist *an sich*, as such, and not as an epiphenomenon, as if only the effect of an absence of good. The evil we know as personal behavior and trait, then, has an importance for Jung that is anchored in his understanding of the psyche as a whole. Our individual evil, our personal shadow, is a reflection of our participation in the nature of things, from top to bottom. Jung's observation concerning evil is *radix*, at the root of his psychological awareness; one cannot understand his view of psyche aside from it.

Jung's thinking on evil carried him into areas that we ordinarily call religious: the transcendent, the trans-personal, the sense of mystery, the more-than-is-obvious that everyone knows, even if off to the side, but rarely thinks of as psychological. Jung's word for the archetypal source, center, and dynamo of psyche is the Self, another sometimes bewildering concept. The Self is an especially difficult term for the English-speaking world, where "self" usually is a reflexive pronoun which effectively means ego, our sense of "I." Jung's meaning includes the "I" in a sense, since the Self is experienced, and it structurally forms the psychological foundation for the ego. Yet it goes far beyond what our casual, even our more precisely academic, use of "self" ordinarily indicates. It is, psychologically speaking, the god-like power—often imaged, always felt—in the unconscious.

Image and emotion announce the presence of the Self in individual life. Plus an awareness that a phenomenon of great personal meaning and importance is taking place. The image together with the emotional power of the presence inevitably incite imagination. Awe might come upon a person, or fear, or astonishment, about which one cannot help but wonder. One is connected, suddenly perhaps, and surprisingly, with a figure, a sound, a perception that bespeaks a more-than-ego authority. One is compelled to pay attention. Jung calls such an experience "numinous," after Rudolf Otto.

The Self appears in collective life as well. Jung believed that the image of Christ has been the culturally central image of the Self in the Christianized world. A crisis in the West, reaching zenith proportions in the twentieth century, for good or for ill, has been the gradual erosion of the power of the Christ image to organize social life. The fatigue of the symbol after two millennia of use, together with the chimera of rational control of life, is an obvious condition of its demise. To wit: it is questionable whether the multitudes who daily file past the Isenheim altarpiece in Colmar see more than an increasingly famous painting. Few weep or rush forth to write. The painting no longer re-presents societal soul. When it does speak, it does so individually, and to an odd and quite personal sensibility.

Here my focus returns to evil—the jarring, incompatible moments when life is wrung away, denied, swept past, squashing desire and hope and valid expectation. Once, a young man on the cusp of professional contribution drove a group to the Newark airport, a distance from Scranton, to collect a friend. On the way back, they stopped to eat. At that point, an inexperienced driver prevailed in her desire to drive, lost control on a curve, hit another car head-on. The original driver, the organizer of the good deed, was killed. Imperfection of life? Incompleteness of life? Surely. Evil, from the viewpoint of human hope, intervened. The promising youth is suddenly gone, evaporated, missing to his parents and brothers forever.

In Jung's view, human frailty is not the fault of humanity; it is a condition of existence. Its roots plunge into the depths of psyche, which perforce includes the Self. Christ, as a symbol of the Self, psychologically encompasses the characteristics of the entire unconscious—including frailty, imperfection, incompleteness, terrible circumstance. My statement at the start of this chapter that Grünewald's crucified Christ in the Isenheim altarpiece suggests that nothing known to the human race is unknown to Christ reflects Jung's understanding of the Self. To see imperfection as the responsibility of ego places an unbearable burden on humanity. As well, it is a distortion of the god-image.

Grünewald's work can give an enormous sense of relief to bewildered and frightened persons, among whom I count myself. The relief is not based upon one's burden being carried by another. Neither is it based upon ferreting out someone else's responsibility for bad things. Rather, an awareness begins to dawn: the image of God shares with me a common nature; the evil I know as a reality in my own life is intrinsic to reality itself.

Christ becomes a tragic figure, or, better said, his image as painted by Grünewald incorporates within itself the inevitability of paradox. He comes as the innocent lamb; he leaves as the ravaged adult, downed, as is everyone, by the venereal flaw. His image bespeaks majesty juxtaposed with poor, poor woe.

DARK CHRIST: ILLNESS

If Christ's inner connection with evil meets a brick-wall of resistance in conventional minds, the suggestion that his death is marked by an inner pathology seems utterly preposterous. Here we move closer to the fever of phantasmagoria.

Illness is experienced by human beings as evil—as the incarnation of shadow, in Jung's sense. Illness is the sign of the long road down, a portent of the end. In the Isenheim Crucifixion, the corruption of illness is out front and gruesome; the end is not portended, it is present. The emaciated body, the bilious skin color, the distorted hands and feet, the pustules and scabs of infection, the general impression of putrefaction are present in the god-image. Personal dignity is overwhelmed by decay. I am reminded of a pen-and-ink drawing of St. Francis I once owned. Francis, with a look of consummate compassion on his face, held in his arms a dreadful leper whose eyes were blank and dazed, whose skin fell in sheets from a formless face, whose lips hung in shreds. The drawing had power because of the co-presence of graceful mercy and degradation, comeliness and ravage. In that drawing, the opposites of beauty and ugliness were depicted in the two figures. In the Isenheim, Christ contains them within himself.

In Jungian psychoanalytic work, the shadow, the dark side of the personality, is the first of one's unconscious aspects to be exposed and, as Jungians like to say, "integrated." One must work on accepting one's own "illness," the primary step in confronting pretension. Shadow can be misunderstood as only the difficult, yet smallish, idiosyncrasies one seems intent upon hiding for the sake of the ego. The foundations of shadow, however, sink deeply into the unconscious, and a thorough understanding of shadow must extend into something far more pervasive, more disturbing than surface negativity. One catches a glimpse, through an ego-crack, of a vast continent of decay and corruption, primal and unexplored.

In *The New York Times* of 20 January 1989, the day of the Bush inauguration, the shadow side of middle-American achievement was told in an article by Joseph Fried headlined "Life's Nightmare Continues for a Howard Beach Victim." Timothy Grimes was one of three black youths set upon by a dozen bat-wielding white teen-agers in Howard Beach, a white section of Queens, New York, on 20 December 1986. One black was killed by a car on a parkway as he ran to escape. Another was badly beaten.

Grimes got away, but the terror of that night further enveloped him in a nightmare that began long before and shows no promise of ending. As a child, Grimes ate paint chips in his slum apartment, and the lead in the paint damaged his brain, leading to slowness, agitation, aggressive behavior involving assault, robbery, and jail. Grimes's brother in Virginia, the married father of two children, offered assistance after Howard Beach, and Timothy went there to live. In June 1988, Timothy shot his brother in the face during an argument over money, permanently damaging his eyesight.

The Grimes story illustrates the difficulty of "integrating" illness as shadow and shadow as evil. It makes one wonder the more at the audacity of Grünewald's inclusion of disease in his Crucifixion. Can it be that God expresses himself in Timothy Grimes, that God is not only *on the side of* the terribly injured brother, out of largesse, but *is* that brother, out of necessity? The dimensions of the incongruity would be almost beyond the mind's capacity were it not for the likes of Grünewald's fantasy. With it, the sick men at Isenheim are sixteenth-century counterparts of Timothy Grimes. Grimes's actions are repulsive even as were the decaying inmates for whom Grünewald painted his ignominious Crucifixion.

DARK CHRIST: SEXUALITY

After returning to America from my Zürich training, I was at a dinner party. Another guest was a man a few years my junior, a professional person with a fine educational and community-leadership background. In the course of conversation, he turned to me and asked, "What *was* original sin?" I was momentarily taken aback. What, indeed, was it? "Why, disobedience," I said, "the theft of consciousness from the divine. The coming of humanity into self-direction. The leaving behind of innocence." "Not so," he said. "It was sex."

Puberty is, of course, related to the loss of innocence. The awakening of desire, of sexual appetite, and its unrelenting presence and pressure in adult life portend the end of naivete. But to hear this active and admirable man naming the source of his creativity, the exercise of his masculine glory, as "original sin" brought to my mind in a flash the straightness of Western assumptions about the "purity" of Christ. The inner conflict between the Christian demand for sexual purity, on the one hand, and the restless gnawings of natural instinct, on the other, has separated Western humanity from its ancient and natural self-image.

Sexuality, as such, could hardly be sinful. Sexuality is the expression of the second of three foundational instincts which animate the embodied soul: self-preservation, the perpetuation of the species, and (Jung's) individuation. Freud seems to have limited his understanding of sexuality to a concrete, specifically erogenous gratification. Jung ingeniously moved sexuality into metaphor, opening it to spiritual meaning. Jung understood that the basis for life energy was the separation of opposites—as in masculine/feminine—and the never-ending human search for their reunion. Understood physically and instinctually, this life energy is sexuality.

Human beings need a close and living connection with their sexuality. I gingerly connect sexuality with the dark side of Christ because Christian tradition so places it, when Christ and sexuality are connected at all. The influence of Christianity, whether or not one follows it, has unconsciously permeated the attitudinal air of Western society, as in the suspicion of my friend at the dinner party. Human sexuality as instinct is the basis of and is inseparable from creativity, intimacy, and ecstasy, all of which, in their permutations, are

simultaneously concrete and metaphoric.[8] Sexuality opens
into transcendence, to the "more than human," to the divine.
It is, as Eliade has written, a hierophany, a manifestation of
the sacred. That is its power.[9]

Sexuality is obviously as threatening as it is promising.
Revealed in the desirous sideward glance, the fleeting, half-
hidden glimmer of interest, the suggestive remark, the inkling of desire is the suggestion of raw desire. Sexuality is loaded
with implication even in its tiniest hints of presence; the continuum from titillation to abuse is intimated in every erotic
hint. Instinct's darkness manifests itself in sexuality in a spectacular and terrifying manner. Instances of sexual brutality,
selfishness, drivenness, and hurt, of lives empty, stunted, and
shattered are so omnipresent in life that no reader will need
an example in this work. The issue is connecting this kind
of evil with the presence of the divine.

Scripture supports Grünewald's painting a Christ dead
from the exogenous onslaught of his captors. To me, however,
his Crucifixion suggests a death coming from a far deeper
disturbance: endogenous disease. Even more disturbed and
disturbing: the disease, coming from the inside, is a consequence of Jesus' having lived his sexuality, exactly the dark
consequence of love that instinct trails in its wake for mor-
tals, generally, and the men of Isenheim, specifically. Such
a hypothesis is, as I have taken pains to indicate, fantasy–the
discourse of imagination. I stake no claim to its literal truth,
nor need I do so in order to work psychologically with
Grünewald's image. How could it be otherwise, since psyche
is image?

In 1988 I was in St. Paul to dismantle our family home
of some fifty years. I discovered an old Boy Scout compen-

dium with a title like "A Handbook for Boys Becoming Young Men." Aha, I thought. I will see what kind of information I was given at the time of my own entrance. Not a word. Not even old bromides about cold showers, the dangers of time spent alone in one's room, the value of sports.

It was as though burgeoning sexuality did not exist. One presumably was expected to make one's way through cosmic changes without benefit of any explicit guidance whatsoever. There was plenty in the book about church-going and helping older people and the geography of the United States. But not a word about the convulsive mutations of new mystery.

What the Boy Scout handbook did not do is done with vengeance in the Isenheim. The men in the Isenheim hospice could not have been aware that syphilis lurked as a killer within their sexual obedience to nature. Grünewald's Christ is not the gentle shepherd one meets in church. There is no orderly Swiss propriety, no Boy Scout innocence, no Republican family values.

But even with the help of intelligent guidance, a budding teen-ager cannot know the heights to which sexuality carries one, the joy of new life, the delight of personal fulfillment, until it happens. Or the agony of disappointment, the furtiveness of behavior, the savagery of hunger, the betrayal of trust, the onslaught of guilt, shame, and error, until that happens. Along with bliss comes illness, so says Grünewald's Christ. Sexuality involves passion. Suffering is unavoidable. Once one crosses the threshold from innocence, evil is the horizon.

A caveat. I do not mean to confine sexuality to genital activity. Sexuality sets that course, and it can never be divorced from the highly eroticised and fundamentally central reality of genitalia as its focus. But as I am using the term in this work, sexuality ranges far beyond explicit physical intimacy. Sexuality means for a male the experience of owning his phallic nature, which extends throughout his masculine personality. For a woman, inner knowledge of herself as the carrier of new life permeates every aspect of her feminine being. Masculine need for the feminine and the round and feminine need for the masculine and the straight are fundamental elements of human physiological and thus psychological life.

Sexuality is lived in every human connection. Body movements, the reaches of the mind in fantasy, the omnipresence and qualities of emotion are metaphors and carriers of masculine and feminine erotic power. I have seen this in a number of Roman Catholic priests, vowed to celibacy. These men have taken a vow of denial, but they are not asexual. I listen to how they preach, how they function in their work. I observe what they notice, what excites them, the tension in their commitment. When they are connected to themselves as males they are sexual men. Our eyes and spirits meet as one man with another, even though I enjoy a freedom to live a genital life and they do not. However difficult their vow may be, their virility is not obscure.

DARK CHRIST: VULGARITY

That my hypothesis is vulgar there can be no doubt. Vulgarity indicates commonness, something lowly and earthborn, within ordinary reach. That is its quintessential appeal. Appealing also is the colloquial use of "vulgar" as suggesting something burlesque, offensive to good taste, coarse, lacking in cultivation. Precisely because of this, the Grünewald Crucifixion has an astonishing and compelling, if strangely paradoxical, beauty.

The beauty is an ability to stun those who hardly notice the anemically uplifting Christ typically presented by the churches, seemingly untouched by inner conflict and pathos. The beauty is the beauty of pain, the beauty of realizing that the terror one contains within oneself is the terror of the Savior, spent upon the cross. It is the terror of one who has been given a sentence of death due to an illness against which there is no avoidance. It is the terror of the word of a loved one that tells one that there is no longer any love.

Grünewald's Isenheim Crucifixion appeared on the front page of *The New York Times* on Sunday, 13 November 1988. A story told of a group of fifteen Hispanic teen-agers from the South Bronx, a section of New York City that is arguably the most devastated and hopeless slum in the First World. A schoolteacher-artist named Tim Rollins taught the youngsters, many of whom had severe learning and emotional problems, to paint. Rollins called them "the Kids of Survival." A star of the group was Carlito Rivera, learning-disabled and behaviorally intractable when he entered the group at age eleven. Rivera chose Grünewald from a pile of art books on a table and began to copy the Temptation of St. Anthony panel of the Isenheim altarpiece.

For his seventeenth birthday, Rollins took Carlito to Colmar. "I was in shock," Carlito said. "It was like something that just hit me. I never thought in my lifetime I'd get to see it except in books. I was so happy that I felt like crying."

Carlito, my wife, and I have something in common that goes deeper than good taste, refinement, and cultivation. Barbara, well educated in the private school tradition, finds Christian symbolism obvious and generally unmoving. I came to the Grünewald from the plebeian Midwest, an exhausted believer and priest. Carlito entered into the mystery as a slum kid who could not read and who could not sit still in school. Tears from all three. The tears suggest a center that draws from something that goes beyond class difference.

Shortly after my return to Zürich in 1989, I revisited Colmar and the Isenheim with Peter, my visiting friend from New York mentioned earlier. Peter, like Barbara, is properly bred and impeccably educated. I came to know him when he was attracted to St. Clement's, the avant-garde New York congregation where I was vicar from 1965 to 1975. His enthusiasm for Christianity burst into flame in those years; today only embers of that enthusiasm remain. Enroute from Zürich to Colmar, Peter and I drove through the Black Forest in dazzling sunshine. As we entered Alsace, penetrating cold and a mid-January pea-soup fog enveloped us. That, together with the empty and unheated Unterlinden Museum, was an altogether appropriate setting for his first approach to the Grünewald Crucifixion. We sat on that same bench Barbara and I had used seventeen years earlier, dumb and overwhelmed. We endured the chill as long as we could, having spent ourselves in the silence of recognition before the painting. We did not so much as look at Colmar, even what we might have seen in the fog. We quietly crept back to Zürich.

Later I asked, "Was it as much as you had expected?" "God, much more. Grünewald put his hands under the pain of the world and lifted it up into the crucifixion. Nothing I've ever seen of Christ is so evocative. Grünewald did in painting what Blake did in writing."

Peter had read my thesis several times in the years after Zürich, and we'd talked of it often. Peter expounds; he encloses whole cultures with a manic sweep of his arm, with a roar of, say, pidgin Russian. Peter feels in a way few men I know feel. Masculine feeling with temper and muscle and intelligence is rare. This time I understood Peter's exaggeration. He was touched in his bone-marrow. Grünewald was in league with his beloved Pasternak, Joyce, and Homer.

Vulgarity—that which flies in the face of the canons of conventional decency—becomes searing beauty in the Isenheim Crucifixion. The common anguish of humankind is incorporated into an image of a man that is an image of God. The longer one contemplates the painting the more vivid is the impression of degradation. The highest image, it begins to occur to one, contains also the lowest—the most sublime, the most despised. One comes for a moment into personal contact with a mystery wrenching in its intensity. The image tumbles rational expectation into a vortex of "shock," as Carlito said. The cultural overlay of decency is demolished.

Shock always moves ego, the point of religious experience. I understand the shock and the tears of Carlito as the shock and tears of self-recognition, as powerful as the wonder of actually visiting the masterpiece an ocean away. Barbara's and my tears did not come from our astonishment at seeing in person what we'd observed in books. We shed no tears at seeing *Mona Lisa* in Paris or *David* in Florence. My emotional response certainly came from the mental image I had carried since seminary times of a Christ plagued by a sexually transmitted disease. But not Barbara's. She carried no such image, and she is not a person who weeps over someone else's image, especially her husband's. Her tears, as mine, came from Grünewald's theophanic accomplishment: his depiction of ugliness, inner evil, the bad luck of contagion, incorporated into the sacred figure.

DARK CHRIST: ALCHEMY

Vulgarity, mixed into the highest image of Christian devotion in Grünewald's Crucifixion, is a mingling of poison and prescription. Alchemy–the work of medieval, pre-scientific chemists who sought to distill pure essence from common stuff–is inescapable as a reference point.

In words that apply to the Grünewald work, Jung wrote,

> . . . [the soul] falls victim to the delusion that the cause of all misfortune lies outside. . . . On the contrary [the soul] has the dignity of an entity endowed with consciousness of a relationship to Deity.[10]

In the simplest of terms, Jung's statement suggests that each individual soul–that is to say, the deepest and most subjective factor of a person's being–has a connection with God as a given characteristic. That conviction was not original with Jung, however surprising it might sound coming from a twentieth-century psychiatrist. A long spiritual tradition holds that the soul's connection with God is the common thread in all mystical awareness, from the first moment that some person, somewhere, knew that he or she was in contact with transcendent reality. The startling element in Jung's conviction is his recognition of the natural wisdom of ordinary, common people. It suggests that a paradoxical dignity is inherent in that which is vulgar.

In his fascination with alchemy, Jung sensed that common earth and dung, the vulgar product of animal digestion, were the *prima materia*, the source material, in the container– the retort–of an individual's life experience. The medieval alchemist believed that, after the contortions of heating and cooling, adding and subtracting, the banal original stuff had the capacity to be seen as the great goal of the laboratory work, the philosopher's gold. Gold, the most precious metal, then, was an inherent, if hidden, property of dung–the most vulgar of rubbish, the effluent, the ordinary, the base. This is what every farmer has always known.

Greatness is concealed within the sweltering, heaving capacity of that which is considered, by consciousness, to be worthless and altogether disposable. This was Jung's revolutionary understanding of psyche. Were dung to stay in the form of decomposed waste matter, unused and despised, it would be dismissed and turned away from, as we easily do. Dumped into rivers and oceans, where it does not belong, it spreads putrefaction. But dung, put upon the earth as fertilizer, becomes an enricher of vegetation, an essential contributor to the health of new growth. So also with the discard of human lives. The inferior–and interior–contaminants of psyche are the means by which life is fed and grows.

Jung wrote, "if the soul no longer has any part to play, religious life congeals into externals and formalities."[11] In Jung's understanding, psyche requires the presence of dung in the compost heap of alchemical transformation. The alchemists lived in an agrarian world, accustomed to spreading waste upon the earth in order to fructify it, converting feces into food. We think ourselves superior, but we, diminishing soul, infect our fields with chemical insecticides and fertilizers—products of ego—poisoning the earth and diminishing the nutrient value of crop. The lettuce we eat might last longer and be fuller, but the danger is that it is saturated with an even more lethal form of untransformed corruption. It is not only religion that stiffens when it attends to appearance. Without an interiority, life shrinks everywhere about us. We are so caught up in our artifice that we fail to notice our diminishment.

As in religion, so in psychotherapy. One can get hold of oneself through treatment and diminish bad behavior. But the improvement may have a deleterious effect upon the quality of life. "Externals and formalities," in the words of Jung, are corrections of appearance, a product that looks better at the supermarket. Lettuce may look green because research has found how to implant green into lettuce, but nutrition is not there. Not so different from a religious functionary "turning out" good children according to formulae—not knowing him- or herself, to say nothing of knowing the chemistry of the students. Interiority shrinks. Therapists, clergy, gurus, teachers, parents who have not found, or even worried that they have not found, the route from dung to gold have a way of turning incipient gold to dung. What might have been a fluid process congeals, stagnates. One gets hardness of heart, disruption of life, psycho- and socio-pathology.

Alchemical metaphor, psychologically understood, is not clean. Its vulgarity cuts through the facade of good manners, plunging into dirt, distress, ontological shadow. Alchemy encircles evil, inhales evil, substantiates evil, which is why Jung was so taken with it. Alchemy is impossible without decomposition, the smell of rot, the harshness of impurity. One might think that, ah, well, the point of the work is gold; the dross, at some point, is left behind. For a moment is that so. The gold is glimpsed, held closely, enjoyed, as with all soul food. But its moment of ripeness slips away or it is consumed. Then the process begins again in the compost heap. The circle is neverendingly repetitive because the opposites never are static. The integration of shadow—both minor and major league—is beguiling, given the ego's propensity for illusion. We want away with filth; yet as we hide from it, it returns to confound us. Our surprise expresses our naivete.

I return to Robertson Davies' novel *The Manticore*. The psychoanalytic patient, Staunton, remembers an event of his youth. With several other boys, he visited a friend, Unsworth. On a lark one day, the group drove far into the forest to a summer cottage owned by an elderly couple not at home. At the instigation of Unsworth, they broke into the house and, falling into a kind of maniacal destructive rampage, proceeded to tear it apart. The frenzy was concluded by Unsworth's gathering together in one place the personal mementos of the couple, mostly family photographs, and defecating on them. Staunton remembered saying to himself,

"Why is he doing that? . . . . It is a dirty, animal act of defiance and protest against—well, against what? He doesn't even know who these people are. There is no spite in him against individuals who have injured him. Is he protesting against order, against property, against privacy? No; there is nothing intellectual, nothing rooted in principle—even the principle

of anarchy–in what he is doing. So far as I can judge–and
I must remember that I am his accomplice in all but this,
his final outrage–he is simply being as evil as his strong will
and deficient imagination will permit. He is possessed, and
what possesses him is Evil."[12]

A gripping, if prankish, example of evil's backing in–
not just a prank to that guileless couple, one might guess.
An outrageous, stupid encroachment, to be sure, a micro-
intrusion of dark presence. Evil was there to be done, appearing in Unsworth and in the other boys, more extreme in one,
less so, perhaps, in the others. Staunton intellectually waxed
on about Unsworth's excesses, but Staunton went along with
the game until his sensibilities were breached, as do we all.
The story reminded me of Jung's recollection of his childhood
"unthinkable thought"–his fantasy of God dropping turds
on the roof of the Basel Cathedral.[13] The bad stuff essentially
belongs along with that which we value and treasure, whether
or not we can explain or stomach it.

We associate the notions of common earth, dung, and
evil through the motif of that which is worthless, vulgar,
destructive. Dross sidles up and pushes us close to our greatest
fear–mortality–when breath clogs and our presence comes
near to *prima materia*. Body–soul connection, as we know
it, sunders. Sickness and death, from the vantage point of
ego-desire, are enemy, the apogee of shadow. Our fear flows
from a knowledge that the end will come, inexorably. The
apocalyptic notes of our anxiety are inherent in the alchemy
of a sacred figure suffering an internal weakness, a *metanoia*,
a recollection, a memory that comes not from explicit experience but from archetypal placement. One's body of aware-

ness changes, goes through a metamorphosis, as in Grünewald's painting of the body of Christ in limitation.

DARK CHRIST: GNOSIS — SECRET KNOWLEDGE

My fantasy with Grünewald's Isenheim Crucifixion bears
a resemblance to gnostic claims for the validity of subjective
and secret, that is, esoteric, knowledge.

Jung examined the psychological significance of gnosis,
particularly its emphasis upon private knowledge. His impetus
came from his extraordinary respect for and interest in the
arcane notions and phenomena which emerged from the unconscious in his patients and in himself. As the romantic
thinker he was, Jung did not dismiss the peculiarities of visions or the visionary, nor did he assume them to be
pathological. I use "romantic" to describe Jung in a philosophical sense, as denoting one who gives structural importance to feeling and mood, to a knowledge of the heart, to
meaning, to theophany, as opposed to the rational legacy of
Descartes' "Cogito, ergo sum."

Jung claimed to be scientific and empirical in his investigation of the psyche, but he was not in the modern sense of
demonstration by laboratory replication. He meant by his
claim that he took with utmost seriousness the phenome-
nology of psychological *experience*, including the oddity of images as they appear in apparently self-determined ways. It is
important to note that in physics, the most radical and
abstract of the modern scientific disciplines, post-Einsteinian
development is remarkably compatible with Jung's intuitive
notions of the psychoid nature of the archetypes and of the

material world: that matter is essentially psyche-like and that psyche is essentially material.

Private and secret knowledge always stands in contrast to convention. Gnostics, in the early years of the Christian era, were separated from the formal body of the Church both by their personal peculiarities and by formal rejection. Subjective knowledge was considered to be incompatible with revealed and collectively acknowledged truth, much as it is today. I myself have no interest in a disputation with creedal proclamations. I have moved from a wrenching contemplation of the Grünewald Isenheim Crucifixion to worship at mass in the Colmar Cathedral without any sense of inner incongruity, however heterodox my gnostic grasp of the painting might be. My receiving communion was a gnostic act in keeping with my personal experience with the painting, requiring, for me, expression within Christian ritual.

First of all, in the Isenheim Crucifixion, gnosis is related to Grünewald's painting a Christ with gross bodily disfigurations, a strange and radical departure from tradition. Since other crucifixion paintings imputed to Grünewald are mild by comparison, I am led to believe that he painted the Isenheim with a special purpose in mind, related to the illness of the Isenheim hospital's patients. Such an intention, while objectively constellated by the painting's hospital use, was also clearly personal on the part of the artist and, in all probability, deeply connected to his own subjective experience. Grünewald's message might have been recognized subliminally by the sick men who attended mass as a communication having to do with the aura of pestilence within which they lived. It had to do with the mass as well, but not simply as a repetition of that which could be found in any Catholic chapel. One cannot tell, of course, what Grüne-wald's inner connection to the altar sacrifice might have been. Here, once again, imagination must make a leap. The transformation of bread and wine into the body and blood of Christ centralizes the Christian cultus upon the moment of the Savior's deepest pain and public reflection. It provides a wide opening for correlation between a patient's (or an artist's) suffering and that of the divine.

Secondly, gnosis plays a part in every emotional experience, actually or potentially. Emotions are never intentional; they present themselves to us, unbidden and with authority. When a door to the unconscious is suddenly opened, one's ego can be caught in a stressful, even threatened emotional downdraft. How one attends to an onrush of emotion indicates one's connection to feeling as a function of the personality. If one is unconnected, emotion is spent in one form or another of concretistic projection. If one is connected, however, literalization can be intercepted by an inner authority that draws one's attention and demands that care be taken with the surge of energy that emotion produces. Emotions are signs that everyone has a capacity for personal and private experience, that everyone has a potential relationship to soul. In this sense, soul-connected emotion is gnostic subjectivity. Gnosis is present in every personal response to the Isenheim.

Even as I write this, in a small hotel by Lake Zürich, a workman blasts a boat with water in his next-door shop, filling my ears and head with jarring sound. The noise shatters my equilibrium, rattles my brains. The serenity of the lake, the trees, the glorious August sunshine, the precious free time—all are jumbled into a cacophony of disturbance. If only

that god-damned noise would stop! Do I wonder if I am upset
by the difficulty of writing about inner illness, with its vein
into the bowels of reality? No. It is the proximity of my room
to that man and his seemingly endless abrasion of quiet. That
is the sweet temptation of literalization. I am failing a test
of feeling differentiation. I am losing soul. It is sifting through
my fingers like sand.

Mountains of reflection upon what draws one's attention
must intervene if another process is to work, a process that
intercepts literalization and finds meaning in symbolization.
The less reflection, the more limited I am by my surface im-
pressions. But whether I reflect or not, the unconscious insinuates itself through the onslaught of the world and my
personal emotional response. I find that the outer vibrations,
as in the blasting man, often enough correspond to an inner
turmoil, bordering, sometimes, on chaos. I want to avoid
that chaos even as I write about it and ponder running to
the hotel desk with complaint. My anxiety rises with the
thought of a wasted day. But, ah, the blasting stops. Although
my ears ring, a modicum of quiet returns.

What happened to me is what so often neutralizes imagination. The symptom passes and once again I have my illusion of peace. Similarly, people stare and are moved or vaguely
discomforted, without knowing why, before the Isenheim
Crucifixion. They move on to lunch. The secret knowledge,
seeping up as from a steaming pot below, is a secret even from
themselves.

Thirdly, to talk of a gnostic-like Grünewaldian secret is
to tell of a sympathy between myself and the painting. The
personal connection I have with the Isenheim has subjective
psychological validity – it is itself a religious experience. And

here I speak not of the Grünewald per se, or of what others have written about it, but of the power of my fantasy about the Grünewald, which finds little place to live and grow in a world dominated by empirical reality. The value of the fantasy is, of course, personal, but it is also more than personal. It might also be genuinely transpersonal and therefore touch upon an objective reality that I experience subjectively. Of this I am certain: the gnostic process is a sound and legitimately psychological approach to religious awareness. All sorts of bumps along the road—neurotic hangups, spurious intentions, developmental shortcomings—can be included in one's perceptive apparatus without reducing the authenticity of a subjective experience.

I have a propensity to respect what goes on inside Carlito, who sees, in a land far from the South Bronx, Grünewald's actual painting, whose reproductions have been his inspiration. As he tells it, Carlito's experience with the Isenheim seems to me to be numinous to him. But there are questions. Why is it numinous for one person and not another? What happens within Carlito—and not within those who go on, having seen another sight, to their *choucroute garni*—that brings him to the threshold of reverence?

I call the shock that Carlito speaks of on seeing the Isenheim a gnostic connection. It is a particular piece of personal knowledge emerging from his inner being, making Carlo the person and the artist that he is. That paintings by slum kids sell for thousands of dollars in New York's art market is the incongruity that prompts a reporter to go after the story and an editor to put the story on the front page of *The New York Times*. But what of me, the reader? I am fascinated by an aspect that many readers will quickly forget. I wonder if

45

Carlito, from the South Bronx, reacted to the Isenheim in a way similar to my fascination, as a revelation. I, from middle-class St. Paul, coming to Grünewald via a far different conglomerate of age, family, education, and professional orientation, connect with Carlito across the distance of a printed report. My fantasy, my hypothesis, hungrily seeks to meet him in his awe. Might our secrets be similar?

That is how I understand everyday gnosis. Gnosis shared is the conjunction of one person's personal knowledge with another's, in their likeness, in the secret jumping of the boundaries of secret. Secret, on the one hand, gives me a certain inner power, bringing me into touch with mystery. On the other, it diminishes my adaptation to outer reality, making me feel strange. The life-giving power of gnosis, seen from the perspective of soul, comes from the authority it conveys. The self-doubt of the gnostic lies in the difficulty of maintaining inner knowledge in the face of popular dismissal. Dismissal is too slight a word. One might call it repulsion or any of a plethora of impediments prompting the fear that comes as a subjective deterrent to my private knowledge. To be strange excludes me from belonging. I am told by the voice of authority—be it inner, as the super-ego in Freud or the negative-father in Jung, or outer, as the bourgeoisie in capitalism or official doctrine in Christianity—that I am wrong.

Introjected exterior authority becomes an interior psychological stone wall, inhibiting my freedom of imagination. All non-personal authorities conspire to establish a certain truth as valid for everyone. The ego, seeking security, feels obligated to obey; my secret then is seen as the enemy. I become normopathic.[14]

Personal knowledge—gnosis—is inherent in subjective

psychological reality, in soul reality. The raw material of gnosis is that which a mother brings into counseling, "knowing" that a child is on the wrong track; she feels it in her bones. It is the clarity with which a wife suddenly "sees" that her husband does not love her. Gnosis begins with the truth a child "understands" about a parent which the parent unintentionally discloses through a revealing, if accidental, word or look. Gnosis arrives on the one day a faithful parishioner decides, after hearing the same sermon forty times, that he will no longer go to church. Gnosis is an inner picture becoming apparent, a coming together, a cohesion of feeling. Once one knows, there can be no turning back without ruining the work of a life. Scales have fallen from one's eyes.

Gnostic significance emerges in the honor given to my inner thoughts, inner constructions, intuitions. They come autonomously and unbidden as emotions do and are experienced as my personal truth. In church, the secret meaning I bring to worship separates me from established explanations and from the laissez-faire attitude of other members. (That is, until I find "Carlito" in the next pew! Catch him; he probably won't be there for long.) Everyday gnosis is the voice within to which I increasingly listen, and carefully speak, with growing respect. Gnosis interferes with the status quo. It is always tinged with danger; off-the-wall, it inflates, isolates, and is proximate to madness. Danger gives an inner secret its power and attraction. Danger is inseparable from archetypal authenticity.

Early on, Jung wrote an odd monograph called "The Seven Sermons to the Dead," in which he spoke in the fictitious voice of a second-century gnostic teacher Basilides, expounding truths revealed by a god named Abraxas. The work later became an embarrassment to Jung himself, to say nothing of his more conventional followers. To me, it is Jung at his secret best. In the fifth sermon, he wrote:

Man shall know that which is smaller,
Woman, that which is greater.
. . . Man shall call spirituality Mother,
Enthrone her between heaven and earth;
He shall name sexuality Phallos and shall place
it between himself and the earth.
For the Mother and the Phallos are superhuman demons
and manifestations of the world of the gods.
They are more effective for us than the gods because
they are nearer to our own being.

When you cannot distinguish between yourselves on the
one hand, and sexuality and spirituality on the other,
And when you cannot regard these two as beings above and
beside yourselves, then you become victimized by them,
i.e., by the qualities of the Pleroma.

Spirituality and sexuality are not your qualities.
They are not things which you can possess and
comprehend. On the contrary, these are mighty demons,
manifestations of the gods and therefore they tower
above you and they exist in themselves. One does not
possess spirituality for oneself and sexuality for
oneself. Rather, one is subject to the laws of
spirituality and sexuality. Therefore, no one escapes
these two demons. They are common causes and grave
dangers, and above all like the terrible Abraxas.[15]

Basilides' words apply to my approach to the Isenheim Crucifixion. He teaches that sexuality and spirituality are both godlike and function in human beings in both beneficent and demonic ways. They are autonomous entities and cannot be controlled by determination. Quite the opposite: they are the force and we are controlled by them. They victimize us as well as bless us; they divide us as well as bring us together. It is foolish to think of their godlike power as only good. Both sexuality and spirituality are also savage, driven attributes by which we participate in the Pleroma, the fullness of divine nature. We can sometimes maneuver the ego's response to instinct (and I include Jung's contribution of individuation as instinct), but we are deluded if we think that we are in control of our deepest needs.

Man discovers spirituality as related to Mother, the heavenly goddess; his sexuality is earthy and grounded: phallic. Woman, although not quoted in the passage above, is truly sexual in relation to the heavens; her spirituality is earthy and partakes of Phallos. Both the heavenly Mother and the earthy Phallos are gods; neither is superior to the other. But man and woman relate to them in opposite ways. Human beings are out-of-touch if they believe ego to be superior to either sexuality or spirituality, whether constellated by the power of heaven or the power of earth. Both are supernatural, the Pleroma. Both tower above and descend far below ego. As Jung (Basilides) knew and wrote: "One [the ego] is subject to the laws of spirituality and sexuality. They exist in themselves. No one escapes."

What Jung wrote about in this early fantasy, and what the Isenheim Crucifixion radically sets forth, is that sexuality is the opposite side of spirituality's coin and is also sacred.

Each is terrible. The terror that spirituality and sexuality inspire in us comes from their coexistence in divine nature, a power that can devour human beings as well as bless them. The ravaged figure on Grünewald's cross is the more aweful as he participates in and expresses both heaven and earth.

2

GRÜNEWALD: THE MAN AND HIS TIME

THE ALTARPIECE TODAY

THE ISENHEIM ALTARPIECE NOW STANDS MAJESTICALLY IN THE Unterlinden Museum in the center of Colmar, Alsace, near the French–German border. It is a huge work, divided into twelve panels that originally opened as pages in a book, covering, when closed, exposing, when opened, the reredos above a high altar. Such an altarpiece is technically called a polyptych. The museum once was a Dominican convent, and the place of honor within the former chapel–a spacious, austere room with clear glass windows–is given over to the altarpiece. The panels are now separated, mounted on either side of two pedestals standing parallel to one another in the center of the chapel. At the end of the space, in what was once the sanctuary area, stand the carved figures of the reredos by Nicholas Hagnower, before and around which the altarpiece was hung. The central figure in the reredos is a seated St. Anthony; on the patron's right stands St. Augustine and on his left, St. Jerome. Beneath them is a carving of the Last Supper.

The outer panels–what one would have seen were the polyptych closed in its original setting–are the Crucifixion, painted on two large hinged central panels which open, and, flanking it, two stationary side panels: St. Sebastian on the viewer's left, St. Anthony on the right. The Entombment of Christ is beneath them. Were the polyptych opened, the next layer would be the Annunciation on the left, the Virgin and Child with the Choir of Angels in the center, the Resurrection on the right. (The Annunciation and Resurrection are currently mounted on the back side of the Crucifixion pedestal.) Opening the Virgin and Choir panels exposed the reredos, with the St. Anthony/St. Paul the Hermit panel on the left and the Temptation of St. Anthony panel on the right. (At present, the Virgin and Choir are mounted on a second pedestal, with the SS. Anthony and Paul and Temptation panels on the reverse side, parallel to the Crucifixion/Annunciation/Resurrection pedestal.)

One is immediately impressed by the integrity between the altarpiece and its containing space, suggesting the original purpose of the paintings as the focus of the Isenheim monastery hospice chapel.

THE ANTONIANS AND THE HOSPICE

The Isenheim altarpiece was commissioned by the *Bruder des Hl. Antonius* for the chapel of its monastery and hospice for sick men at Isenheim, twenty-five kilometers south of Colmar.

According to tradition, St. Anthony the Hermit, patron of the Brothers, was born in Koma, Egypt, in 251 and died at the age of one hundred five in 356. His parents were wealthy nobility and converts to Christianity who died when Anthony was eighteen years of age. At twenty, he gave his inheritance to the poor and dedicated himself to austerity, prayer, and meditation. He became a desert recluse, and word spread of his thaumaturgic powers, of his fearlessness against the devil, demons, and wild animals. He is generally considered to be the founder of Christian eremitical monasticism.

During the Crusades, the Count of Dauphiné brought St. Anthony's bones to France, where they are purported to remain to this day in the church of Motte-au-Bois near Vienne. As epidemics raged in the Dauphiné, pilgrimages were made to the saint's shrine and miraculous cures became known. About 1090, a rich nobleman of the Dauphiné, Gaston, and his son Gerin were among those who sought help from Anthony. Gerin was a victim of the Holy Fire, and Gaston vowed that if his son were healed he would give his wealth for the benefit of other sufferers. Gerin did recover, Gaston fulfilled his promise, and both he and his son became nurses. They founded a hospital brotherhood; St. Anthony's name was given to the order and to the disease which the brothers sought to alleviate.

The brothers remained faithful to their original task and became known and respected as organizers and administrators of hospitals which specialized in only one sickness, St. Anthony's Fire. Around 1300, the Isenheim hospice was established. Isenheim was an unimportant little town, as it is today, but it lay on the main road from Mainz to Basel, the route from the Rhineland to Italy. A paper dating from 1480 tells that so many pilgrims would spend the night in Isenheim that often "a third Mass had to be said."[1] It was for a refuge for sick men, however, that Grünewald painted his altarpiece.

The Antonians left Isenheim in 1777,[2] and eventually they disappeared as a community, as did their Isenheim hospice. *The New Catholic Encyclopedia* gives no information about them. One can speculate that they were swept away in the anti-religious waves of the French Revolution. It is probable, too, that they had already found the need for their services waning. They were a single-minded community devoted to combating a specific medieval malady. At the time of the French Revolution, the altarpiece was removed from Isenheim, hidden away to prevent its destruction, and subsequently established at the Unterlinden in Colmar in 1852. During World War I, the altarpiece was moved to Munich for safekeeping during the Alsatian battles, returning to Colmar in 1919. During its Munich sojourn, it became widely known and celebrated by German scholars as a national masterpiece.

WHO WAS GRÜNEWALD?

The Historical Puzzle

The altarpiece was executed, probably in the years 1512–15, by a German painter who came to be known as Mattias Grünewald. There is considerable unclarity about the real name of the artist; Grünewald has become firmly attached to him through common usage. The altarpiece was commissioned by Guido Guersi, preceptor of the Isenheim Antonian house from 1490 until his death in 1516. It is not known how or why he chose Grünewald.[3]

Grünewald, the man, is almost a complete mystery. Only the barest outlines of his life may be sketched, even after a century of painstaking research which still continues. Four of the fifteen addresses given at the Grünewald symposium sponsored by the Centre National de la Recherche Scientifique held in Strasbourg and Colmar in October 1974 concentrate on the question of Grünewald's identity, while a number of others touch upon it. Everything one reads about Grünewald speaks to this problem and what might be conjectured about him from an examination of his work and his time.

The name Mattias Grünewald first appeared in a sourcebook on early German art compiled after the middle of the seventeenth century by Joachim von Sandrart entitled *Teutsche Academie*, being inserted only when the book was in the press. According to Eberhard Ruhmer, von Sandrart got the name "from an obscure source."[4] Previously, Grünewald was known as Mathis von Oschnaburg (Aschaffenburg) and was credited as being the artist of the Isenheim altarpiece as early as 1573 by Bernhard Jobin. Ruhmer wrote that

. . . the altarpiece is mentioned in French sources as a work by Dürer . . . and as such it was regarded during the whole of the XVIII century. . . . At the beginning of the XIX century Sulpiz Boisseree began to doubt Dürer's authorship. . . . [Yet] in 1820 C. M. Engelhardt considered the Isenheim altarpiece to be a collective work of Dürer and Grünewald, attributing to the latter the *Crucifixion*, the *Annunciation*, the *Resurrection* and the *Entombment*. . . . Jacob Burckhardt was the first to reclaim the entire altarpiece for Grünewald (Stuttgart Kunstblatt, 1844). . . .[5]

According to Michael Meier, Grünewald was known to his contemporaries as Mathis the Painter, Mathis von Seligenstadt, or von Wurzburg, or as Dürer called him on the occasion of their only meeting at the coronation of

Charles V in Aachen in 1520, simply Mathes.[6] Arthur Burkhard considers von Sandrart's choice of the name Grünewald ("Green-wood") "an unintelligent invention." In common with many Grünewald scholars, he believes that only the artist's first name is accurate. It was variously recorded as Mathis(es), Matt(h)ias, and Matthaeus. His family name was probably Gothardt (Gothart), to which a second name, Nithardt (Nithart/Neithardt/Neithart), perhaps the maiden name of his wife, was sometimes added.[7] Three signatures generally regarded as authentic – on the frame of the altar of *St. Mary of the Snows* in Aschaffenburg, on the *St. Lawrence* in Frankfurt, and on the drawing of the *Three Mens' Heads* in Berlin – combine the initials M–G–N in several ways. This has led to the conclusion that some combination of the names Mattias–Gothart–Nithart was probably in use.[8] That such obscurity and reticence – even invisibility – has significance from a psychological point of view can hardly be doubted.

Grünewald may have been born in Wurzburg and served an apprenticeship there before establishing a residence as a young man in the nearby village of Seligenstadt. Burkhard, after much consideration, postulates a birthdate ca. 1475(6). It is known that Grünewald died in Halle in August 1528. If these dates are correct, Grünewald lived some fifty-three years, and he and Dürer were exact contemporaries.

Grünewald was employed as artist-in-residence at the court of Uriel von Gemmingen, Archbishop of Mainz, from 1508 to 1514, and by his successor, Cardinal Archbishop Albrecht von Aschaffenburg, who concurrently held the sees of Brandenburg, Mainz, and Halle. It is known also that between 1511 and his death in 1528 Grünewald worked in Frankfurt, Oberissigheim, Mainz, and Halle, and that he was involved in some business dealings with a Master Michael Wesser of Altkirk, Alsace, near Basel, from 1513 to 1518. Those were the years in which Grünewald painted the altarpiece at Isenheim, just north of Altkirk. It is unlikely that he traveled farther from his Rhine River homeland than this.

According to von Sandrart, as reported by Ruhmer, Grünewald "lived a solitary and melancholy life and was unhappily married."[9] His marriage took place late in his life, probably after the completion of the Isenheim altarpiece. His wife brought into the marriage a son, Andre(a)s, whom Grünewald adopted.[10] Grünewald was himself childless, a fate he also shared with Dürer. His final years were spent in Halle, as he had been dismissed by Cardinal Albrecht, at first a Lutheran supporter, later an opponent. This appears to be a demotion due to Grünewald's sympathy with the Peasants' Revolt of 1525, which Albrecht strongly opposed. Grünewald appears to have been interested in the teachings of Luther, whose translation of the Bible and printed tracts were found in his effects after his death. This would not have endeared him to Albrecht, who became a strong supporter of the preaching of the Indulgence by Tetzel—a spark that set off the Reformation.

Meier attributes to Grünewald a testimony that he "unfortunately had not accomplished a great deal."[11] If Grünewald was referring to his entire life (and he might have been, as a will was found in Frankfurt after his death), it is a telling self-evaluation indicating an unawareness of his own genius. That, or an involuted false modesty. Withal, the statement points to the veil behind which he hid and the successful efforts he appears to have made to outwit the nigh equal determination of Grünewald scholars to unearth the smallest details about his life. The enigma of Grünewald is congruent with the mystery that fascinates one on encountering his Isenheim masterpiece.

Grünewald left no writings except the will. He had not even a consistent signature. He did, however, leave work. Yet the question of authenticity in this area is as great as in his personal history. Burkhard suggests the following paintings as genuine, a list (with their present locations) generally accepted by sources at my disposal:

1503	Lindenhardt Altar (Lindenhardt)
c. 1505	Mocking of Christ (Munich)
c. 1508	Crucifixion (Basel)
1511	St. Cyriac and St. Lawrence (Frankfurt)
+ 1516	Isenheim Altarpiece (Colmar)
1519	Stuppach Madonna [St. Mary of the Snows] (Aschaffenburg)
1519	Founding of St. Maria Maggiore (Freiburg)
1520	Small Crucifixion (Washington)
1522	Crucifixion (Karlsruhe)
1523	Christ Bearing the Cross (Karlsruhe)
1523	St. Maurice and St. Erasmus (Munich)
+ 1525	Mourning over the Body of Christ (Aschaffenburg)[12]

(+ = before)

A number of drawings and sketches exist, some of which have been found only recently and about which arguments wax furiously. Other than these, and a few entries in official records in Frankfurt, Mainz, and Halle substantiating his presence in those places in certain years, nothing of substance has been found. Grünewald simply disappeared.

Interpretive Fantasies

I believe that it is legitimate, even necessary, to speculate about Grünewald psychologically as well as biographically – in a limited way and with care. I do so to imagine how Grünewald the man might have been a vehicle, a conduit, for an influence far greater than, and paradoxically related to, the paucity of what we know about him. His reticence and his long-time public obscurity further beg the question. Grünewald's outer "invisibility" is of psychological importance, a clue to how his ego-effacement might have opened him to the unseen, primal, archetypal world which he captured in his Isenheim altarpiece. A man's work comes out of who he is, how he embodies himself, and how he interacts with the cultural milieu in which he lives.

Erich Neumann, the Israeli Jungian scholar, wrote:

. . . in the creative man we find a preponderance of the archetypal in keeping with his creative nature.

In the life of the creative man (who by his very nature is dependent upon his receptivity toward the creative unconscious), the emphasis always lies on the transpersonal factors; i.e., in his experience the archetypal factor is so predominant that in extreme cases he becomes almost incapable of personal relations.[13]

In Grünewald's avoidance of recognition, perhaps an aspect

of poor personal relations, we discern an entryway for the powerful forces which inspired him as an artist. Grünewald does indeed sound like an extreme case.

Grünewald and Dürer Compared

Comparisons between Dürer and Grünewald began in the sixteenth century and even today show no sign of abating. The two artists are known to have met only once, in Aachen in 1520, yet they were born and lived in the same part of Germany, and each knew of the other's work and reputation. Dürer and Grünewald are different from almost every perspective. Much is known about Dürer—an aid in speculation about Grünewald through comparison and differentiation. Important, as well, is their time—the Zeitgeist of German art and culture at the beginning of a new aeon.

Dürer felt no necessity to back away from the world or to make a mystery of himself. In Panofsky's compendium on Dürer, he notes that the two artists, plus Cranach, were compared by Melanchthon (Luther's advocate), who likened "Dürer's style to the *genus grande* of rhetoric while comparing Grünewald's to the *genus mediocre* and Cranach's to the *genus humile.*"[14]

The impression one gets of Grünewald's self-depreciation seems to fit his long obscurity in the world of German art. Given his extraordinary modesty, it is unlikely that Grünewald noticed his own importance, and if Melanchthon is an indication, his contemporaries did not. Grünewald remained unappreciated until the twentieth century.

As Burkhard put it, writing in 1936:

During the last three decades German critics have finally appraised his extraordinary works with the respect they deserve, and acclaimed with enthusiasm the dynamic personality that produced them.[15] In Germany, at least, Matthias Grünewald is today esteemed important enough to be placed in the same exclusive sphere with Albrecht Dürer, but at the opposite pole, from which prominent position he represents to the world of art, together with Dürer, the two-fold possibility of development in German painting.[16]

In his address before the 1974 Grünewald symposium, Ruhmer called attention to Dürer's "pushing himself forward, in his *herrisch*, commanding, imperious way," feeling himself mentally elite, craving public confirmation and validation, "feeling himself King of the mind and of art."[17] Kenneth Clark, the English critic, called Dürer

intensely self-conscious and inordinately vain . . . . [His self portrait] insists on its sensibility and is a masterpiece of self-love; and two years later he went even further, by portraying himself in the traditional pose and likeness of Christ.[18]

Was this a manifestation of the Renaissance spirit in Dürer mixed with a measure of hubris? Whatever, it was far from Grünewald. Dürer's concentration upon line and form and Italianate proportion – with his travel, tracting, entrepreneurial agility, and self-promotion – marks him as a German with strong cosmopolitan interthreadings. To find the common German soul of the time, one might better look to Grünewald.

It has been suggested that Grünewald painted himself as St. Sebastian on a panel to the side of the Isenheim Crucifixion.[19] However clearly a martyr, St. Sebastian is not Christ. He is passive, an onlooker, tortured by staves. In medieval iconography, spears or arrows can represent the plague, an attack by a malignant spirit, even as in psychoanalytic literature the knives suggest a phallic attack. By so painting himself, Grünewald may have associated himself with victims in the Isenheim hospice, victims of a fate entwined with sexuality—whether they knew this or not—and considered pestilential by the world. Sebastian's face is weak, with a touch of self-pity about it.

Introversion and the "Subjective Factor"

If Dürer was *herrisch*, then Grünewald displays a decidedly introverted public presence. Dürer was inspired and challenged by the Italian Renaissance: he visited Italy at least twice, he knew the famous men of his time and was known by them, and he courted and received international recognition. He knew that he was an important person and painted himself as such. This prominence was aided by his primary medium, the reproducible woodcut, which spread his fame.

Grünewald was very much Dürer's opposite. He never traveled beyond the short distance to Alsace. He was uncommunicative, unheralded; he appears to have had a penchant for anonymity; he may have been a man who lived by himself. He made few efforts to encompass within his work the innovations of the new Mediterranean humanism; he is considered by some critics to be the last of the German Gothic artists. If the cloak of obscurity which covers him were cast aside, one might find a retiring nature, sensitive and fragile, a man in sympathy with outcasts, at home with an other-worldly understanding of his subject. Ruhmer says that "Dürer's attention is focused on this world; Grünewald is awake to the metaphysical." One is pointed in a mystical direction.[20]

How can this be understood psychologically? One can translate Ruhmer's assertion into something like this: Dürer focused his attention upon the outer, so-called object world, while Grünewald was more sensitive to and expressive of something very different, what I have been calling inner and subjective. If so, this calls for an understanding of Ruhmer's "metaphysical" as encompassing that which Jung called

> the subjective factor . . . [which] has, from the earliest times and among all peoples, remained in large measure constant . . . [The subjective factor] is a reality that is just as firmly established as the external object. If this were not so, any sort of permanent and essentially unchanging reality would be simply inconceivable, and any understanding of the past would be impossible.[21]

While one admires the consummate skill, range, and extent of Dürer's work, his incorporation of the new learning, one is moved to tears by the Isenheim Crucifixion. Jung called the subjective factor "ineluctable" for human beings, a fate which cannot be escaped.[22] This is reason to view Grünewald as dominated by his subjectivity and inner world—an introverted man, perhaps extremely introverted, as opposed to Dürer's extraversion.

According to Ruhmer,

Dürer's art is masterly, objective, idealistic, and is good for everybody. Grünewald's highly sensitive art is a special case with all of its imponderabilities. Grünewald doesn't look for the visible, controllable, concrete values—he looks, rather, for the opposite. Grünewald's art is so subjective that it is stylistically not imitatable in a *schulbildung* way. The work of a student of Dürer can be so perfect that you can sometimes mistake it for being Dürer's. A Grünewald imitation is not possible . . . Grünewald has an extreme originality, an unconsidered subjectivity, a profound spirituality.[23]

And, from Erwin Panofsky:

Grünewald was a Christian mystic—no secular representation by him is known—where Dürer, with all his piety, was essentially a humanist. . . . [Grünewald was] a poet [while Dürer] was a scientist in spite of his fervid imagination.[24]

Both Ruhmer and Panofsky bear out my point: Grünewald was dominated by something taking place within himself, by archetypal configurations impinging upon his subjective awareness. Dürer's fascination was with the new humanistic currents of the Italianate Renaissance. It is Grünewald's introverted contact with his inner process, and the convergence of his subjective process with an authentic substratum of archetypal substance, that gives his Isenheim Crucifixion its peculiar and characteristic numinosity. Of course, introversion does not guarantee that a personal experience of numinosity can be convincingly communicated to others. Yet, archetypal patterns lie imbedded in the deepest recesses of psyche, and the introvert has a natural propensity for a personal intimacy with them. Here the psychological difference between Dürer and Grünewald is crucial. Dürer was able to superbly copy what he saw, and in the new mode. Grünewald painted an interior vision.

Zeitgeist

Huysmans claims that Grünewald captured the Zeitgeist in his Crucifixion:

> One might say that he personifies the fierce and pettifogging spirit of the Germany of his time, a Germany excited by the ideas of the Reformation. Was he involved, like Cranach and Dürer, in that emotional religious movement which was to end in the most austere coldness of the heart, once the Protestant swamp had frozen over? I cannot say–though he certainly lacks nothing of the harsh fervour and vulgar faith which characterized the illusory springtide of the early sixteenth century. For me, however, he personifies still more the religious piety of the sick and the poor. . . . It is easy to see why Grünewald's name, unlike the names of Holbein, Cranach and Dürer, is not to be found in the account-books or the records of commissions left by emperors and princes. His pestiferous Christ would have offended the taste of the courts; he could only be understood by the sick, the unhappy and the monks, by the suffering members of Christ.[25]

The Isenheim altarpiece reflects the ambivalence present in Germany approaching the cataclysm of the Reformation. On the one hand, popular fervor surged in support of the political rights of the ordinary man. On the other, medieval

Catholic pietism was intact, forming a cultural and theological basis for society. More so than the other Isenheim panels, the Crucifixion shows a certain Lutheran influence in its emphasis upon the vulnerability of Jesus, a suffering god-image with whom destitute human beings could identify. Grünewald's sympathy with the Peasant's Revolt may also be seen. The theological issue imbedded in the Indulgence controversy was the earning of salvation through individual propitiation, a medieval expression of a dominating, feudal God characterized by love of wealth, power, and control. The Annunciation panel and the Choir of Angels display a traditional Catholic devotion to the Virgin, surrounded as she is by artifacts of royalty. The disjuncture incorporates Grünewald's ambivalent participation in the cultural upheaval of his time.

The grotesqueness of the Crucifixion and the Temptation of St. Anthony panels shows Grünewald's response to the wretched condition of the patients he contacted in his years at the hospice in Isenheim. Some scholars feel that he was also influenced by the *Revelations of St. Birgitta of Sweden*, first published in German in 1492. Birgitta (Bridget) spent her final years in Rome and wrote there of her visions. They contain hideous threats of perdition to be visited upon humankind as a result of the corruption she encountered in the Church. She uses starkly cruel language in her meditations on the crucifixion. Some of her verbal images can be matched with Grünewald's pictorial choices, viz.: "Thou art the Lamb that John pointed out with his finger," and "His feet were curled round the nails as round door hinges towards the other side."[26] In any case, Grünewald expressed his anguished participation in the crisis of Germany by translating a measure of the people's torment into his Crucifixion.

Grünewald's time was one of the great turning points of European history. North of the Alps, the last vestiges of the Middle Ages were drawing to an explosive close. South of the Alps, the same revolution, very differently constituted, was in full flower. The high Renaissance in Italy was the culmination of one hundred years of gradual and organic change.

The difference can be grasped by comparing works painted at the same time as the Isenheim altarpiece – the second decade of the sixteenth century. At that time, Leonardo painted *Mona Lisa*, a Renaissance testament to the "value of earthly life . . . increased and given a significance that is as remote from the Middle Ages as it is from China."[27] Giorgione painted *The Concert*, "absorbed in recreating, through light and color, the beauty of a 'golden moment' when man is completely attuned to the poetic mood of nature."[28] In the North, we find both medieval mysticism and populist suffering. Cranach's *Rest on the Flight into Egypt* is "a tender idyl in a fairy-tale forest."[29] Dürer's engraving *Knight, Death and Devil* (inspired by Erasmus's *Manual of the Christian Knight*) shows "the grimly determined knight in his heavy gothic armor, forging ahead, oblivious of the two rather grotesque terrors that accost him . . . as far removed as possible from the agile intelligence . . . of the great scholar."[30] The Isenheim altarpiece mixes the German old with the German new, medieval faith with the portents of revolution.

Grünewald, unlike his German contemporaries, combined a medieval mysticism with a radically new ground-level social realism in his Isenheim altarpiece. In Italy, artists may have used the images of Christianity, but did so as a means of expressing "a nostalgia . . . to affirm the dignity of man amid the 'wondrous setting out' of a universe shaped . . . with beauty and comeliness."[31] Humanistic idealism did not appear in German works. Ruhmer claims that the difference was due to "the greater flexibility of the clergy in Italy."[32] It cannot have been as simple as that.

Profound discontent characterized Germanic Europe at the turn of the sixteenth century. A rising mercantile class was tearing apart the medieval structure of feudalism, coming hard upon agrarian depopulation due to war, famine, and disease. Growth in the dissemination of information and learning through the founding of new universities, such as Marburg, and the invention of movable type created a general dissatisfaction with the old order. The German artist's *Wanderjahr* took him to Holland as well as to Florence and Venice, where change was taking place. Taxes continued to be levied upon local constituencies by the Roman Church as though it were still the ecclesiastical arm of the Roman Empire. Agents moved back and forth between Germany and Rome with these funds, and stories were told about the people the money supported. Luther went to Rome in 1510 as a young Augustinian friar, and its courtly opulence deeply offended him.

Luther did not intend to rend the Church but to reform it. The intransigence of the popes made this impossible. Don Rodrigo de Borgia, elected pope in 1492 as Alexander VI, "typified, to the highest degree, Renaissance man: he had versatile intelligence, extraordinary energy, boundless ambition, but he was also completely unscrupulous."[33] He was followed by Julius II, who led military expeditions in person to extend the political domain of the Vatican.

Erasmus, in his *Querela Pacis* of 1517, lamented the situation, helping to spread unrest in the North:

What have the helmet and the mitre in common? What connection is there between the crozier and the sword, between the Holy Gospel and the buckler:? How, O bishop, standing in the room of the Apostles, dare you teach the peoples the things that pertain to war?[34]

Julius's pressing the claims of papal absolutism helps one to perceive the background from which the northern revolution grew. Augenas says in the *New Cambridge Modern History*, "at the end of the fifteenth century especially, it was all too clear that the financial needs of the papacy – sometimes for the meanest ends – governed the entire policy of the Roman See."[35]

Julius was succeeded in 1513 by Leo X, a man of refinement, humanity, and flexibility. Yet he failed to discern the danger inherent in even greater taxation. In 1515-16, Tetzel carried on his Indulgence campaign in Germany as a means of raising money to complete St. Peter's in Rome. This proved to be the spark which set Christian Europe ablaze. The controversy which ensued provided Luther with the opportunity he needed to present his ninety-five theses in 1517 in Wittenberg – a constellating factor rather than the root cause of the chaos engulfing Germany. The *Encyclopedia Britannica* states that

the policy of fastening the Church, a universal institution, into the Reich, with its well-defined frontiers, is usually associated with the reign of Otto I (Holy Roman Emperor, 962-73). But it gathered momentum only in the reigns of his successors. Bishops and abbots became competitors of lay princes in the formation of territories, a rivalry which, more than any other, was the fuel and substance of ceaseless feuds, the smouldering internal wars in all regions of Germany for centuries. The welter and confused mosaic of the political map of Germany until 1803 is the not-so-remote outcome of these 10th and 11th century grants and of the incompatible ambitions which they aroused.[36]

It has been claimed that Maximilian I, Holy Roman Emperor from 1493 to 1519, toyed with the idea of nationalizing the German church, while conspiring to get himself elected pope.[37] Such notions underscore the unmooring of traditional relationships and the shifting loyalties which characterized Grünewald's period.

Additional evidence of German restlessness may be seen in the widespread mistrust of Roman law, which ran counter to the romantic nature of German tradition, and a distaste for Italian humanism, which was considered to be based upon an infatuation with paganism. Anger at church functionaries was incendiary—at bishops who were feudal lords and who held multiple benefices (such as Cardinal Albrecht), and at the large numbers of uneducated and careless lower clergy—an anger which broke into flame in the Peasants' Revolt of 1525. This Peasants' Revolt, fed by Luther's agitations, was a rising of German poor against their feudal overlords to protest their increasingly servile condition. The growth of a mercantile class squeezed the aristocracy who squeezed the peasants. Meanwhile, Grünewald remained dependent upon the patronage of the ecclesiastical nobility for his living.

The Germany of Grünewald's time produced the *Malleus maleficarium* (The Hammer of Witches), promulgated in 1487 by the Dominicans Henry Kramer and James Springer of Cologne. Approved by Pope Innocent VIII and Emperor Maximilian I, it "characterizes the spirit of the times"[38] and "became the most horrible document of its age . . . [expressing] a kind of persecutory mania manifested by the Catholic Church and the German state as a means of containing any challenge to their authority and security."[39] If, indeed, Grünewald was moved by Luther, sympathetic to the Peasants' Revolt, drawn to the distressed of the Isenheim hospital, his alliance with outcasts made him an apt instrument for archetypal forces pushing their way toward collective expression. Grünewald expressed in his bizarre interpretations the volcanic upheaval taking place in the German psyche.

The intensity of German excitement at this time has been caught by Kenneth Clark in his comparison of *The Portrait of a Cardinal* by Raphael with Dürer's *Oswald Krell*.

> The cardinal is not only a man of the highest culture but balanced and self-contained. Oswald Krell is on the verge of hysteria. Those staring eyes, the look of self-conscious introspection, the uneasiness, marvelously conveyed by Dürer through the uneasiness of the planes in the modelling—how German it is. . . . [40]

And how well Clark's comparison reveals the strain of German restlessness. While Dürer caught the tension of sixteenth-century Germany in a formal portrait, Grünewald's convulsed Crucifixion mirrored the soul of his people.

Grünewald did not record, as did his contemporaries. He did no benighted peasants, no lovely Renaissance bodies, no portraits of Cardinal Albrecht, Luther, learned doctors, or the new mercantile bourgeoisie, no great battle scenes such as those depicted by Altdorfer. Grünewald's subject matter remained completely within the mythic world of medieval Christianity, skewed by his deeply subjective introversion. His treatment was a confession of his participation in the common plight of human beings. One finds, particularly in the Isenheim Crucifixion, an implicit expression of his own pain and the pain of the German people caught in the grip of a social upheaval of monumental proportions. Because Grünewald was connected to his land and to his own profound introversion, he painted with a strange and perplexing kind of genius. The difference between Grünewald and the average person of his time, who also had access to archetypal experience, was the depth of his subjective encounter, his courage, and his ability to translate his experience into consummate art. Burkhard calls him "the last and greatest artist of the German Middle Ages."[41] Huysmans calls him "the boldest painter who has ever lived."[42] Pevsner calls him the German Correggio in his excitement and sensationalism.[43]

TWENTIETH-CENTURY PARALLELS

Grünewald's sixteenth-century work depicts dimensions of archetypal reality that have not fully entered common awareness in the twentieth century. And, as we today approach the end of a millennium, we also stand at a crossroads, as portentous as that which Grünewald and the German people faced in the sixteenth century. Grünewald has been discovered in the twentieth century because his Isenheim altarpiece speaks to our broken condition.

My work, with its hypotheses concerning evil, sexuality,

and illness in the archetypal realm of the sacred, addresses a part of our current poverty. I point to the need in our day for a god-image – for we will have one, no matter what name we call it – that challenges conventional wisdom, that reaches toward an inclusive range of human experience, that is not the product of public opinion.

Our world continues to be unevenly divided between people who are surfeited with externals and people who not only own nothing, but also marginally survive, if at all. Sexuality is the only pleasure available to hundreds of millions of people, with a consequent explosion of population and disease unimaginable even a generation ago. In the midst of social chaos, Grünewald jolts one into a surprising awareness: paradox, rather than reason, is a guiding principle of psychological truth. It is a message that is remarkably congruent with elements of both Christianity and Jung.

Rich learn from poor, well from sick, intelligent from common. With our world edging closer to a racial, economic, and environmental precipice, the schism between good and evil, mind and soul, matter and spirit engendered by an "enlightened" confidence in human rationality becomes increasingly untenable and dangerous. In Grünewald, a compelling scent of resolution feeds a hunger to investigate its hidden source.

Emma Jung in her life-work *The Grail Legend* wrote of

the curious enantiodromia that, from the year 1000 A.D. on, tended to reassess all Christian contents . . . still dominant in the first half of the fish aeon . . . while the earthy, natural, mortal Anthropos . . . should, conversely, be raised up to the place of the highest guiding principle.[44]

The fish—and Christian—aeon is, with our century, coming to a close. Grünewald lived at the mid-point of its second half. He painted "mortal Anthropos"—or, as I have come to name it, Urperson[45]—in his Isenheim Crucifixion, a concurrence of commonness and universality, ego and Self, expressing the coexistence and omnipresence of good and evil. As the earthy, natural life of instinct returns today to the primal place in Western life from which the Church has sought to dislodge it since the beginning of the Christian aeon, Grünewald's Crucifixion image stands as a possibility of uncomfortable resolution.

Erich Neumann wrote of Grünewald's time that ". . . what actually happened—and it is a phenomenon decisive for this epoch—was a reappearance of the earth archetype, in opposition to the heaven archetype that had dominated the middle ages."[46] The enantiodromia to which Emma Jung referred is a reversal in direction, a turning about of psychic energy, a movement into an opposite. Grünewald was caught by the archetypal evolution to which both Mrs. Jung and Neumann point, and he expressed the change in his piebald painting, anticipating the age of Aquarius by five hundred years.

3

ARCHETYPES

I USE JUNG'S THINKING ABOUT ARCHETYPES AS THE BASIS OF my imagining on the Grünewald Crucifixion. Archetypes are a foundational concept for Jung: he wrote volumes about them and their permutations, as have his followers. This brief and impressionistic introduction is for the reader who is unfamiliar with Jung's archetypal thinking.

By taking his own subjectivity with a radical seriousness, unequaled even today in depth psychology, Jung was plunged into the unconscious and a new world of psychic reality. Jung's remarkable way of looking within himself was extreme. His giving dignity to introversion and introspection, and the products of this search, was fraught with individual peculiarity and pathology. Yet it led him to psychic data that was, paradoxically, objective – an inner counterpart, as it were, to the outer world we all perceive with our senses. And it has led others to trust his way, a way that corroborates a style of knowing that affirms personal experience while it borrows but lightly from generally accepted opinion.

Jung's split with Freud hung on this difference: was the unconscious an epiphenomenon, "an attendant phenomenon appearing with something else and referred to that as its cause,"[1] or was it fundamental, the base upon which the structure of consciousness was individually and collectively constructed?

Jung's doubts about Freud's accuracy in attributing the activity of the unconscious solely to the repression of unacceptable personal material climaxed during their voyage to America in 1909. As recounted in *Memories, Dreams, Reflections*, Jung submitted to Freud a dream involving a subterranean cavern beneath Jung's house which, when explored, revealed Roman ruins and prehistoric artifacts. Freud felt the dream dealt with possible conflicts in Jung's private life. Jung was uneasy. "My dream," he stated in his memoirs, "obviously pointed to the foundations of cultural history—a history of successive layers of consciousness. . . . something of an altogether *impersonal* [and in this sense, objective] nature underlying that psyche."[2]

Thus Jung was prepared to believe early on that a serious delving into the depths of the unconscious might lead beyond what was individually troublesome to that which was psychologically fundamental. By being thoroughly and tenaciously subjective, Jung came upon a dimension of the psyche that is substantively objective and impersonal, even transpersonal. And, paradoxically, personal. For there is no way to the font of transpersonal wisdom without a singular journey, profound and isolating in its subjectivity. This was Jung's new world of psychic reality. The world Jung found cannot be discovered by Freud's causal, reductive method alone, important as this is in discovering where and how the "impersonal nature underlying the psyche" coalesces with one's life experience. Subjectivity, taken to its zenith, also its nadir, introduces one to its opposite. One cannot understand Jung without a grasp of the essential presence of paradox in psyche, as illustrated by this story.

Psyche is the underlayment of all individual experience.

All individual experience is a variation of a prior, psychologically inherited, universal pattern. The pattern can be found, in a life-changing sense, only personally. Jung's notion of a priori pattern is similar to Plato's pre-existent ideas, "archaic . . . primordial types . . . universal images that have existed since the remotest times."[3] Jung called these nodal points of perception and behavior by the ancient Greek term "archetypes." He thus carried psychoanalytic theory a monumental step beyond Freud, for it became inferentially possible, through an exploration of an individual's subjective history and dreams, to discover typical situations and motifs within which the archetypes function in that person's personality. Jung opened a way for psychotherapy to become a modern counterpart to religious initiation, in which one encounters a universal dimension of meaning in one's life. Analytical Psychology thus became more than a medical discipline for cure. It became a means of discovering spirit and soul.

Jung called the objective realm of patterns in psyche the collective unconscious, as opposed to the personal unconscious, the forgotten and repressed experiences of the individual. Archetypes, the universal patterns, emerge in individual and social history through and within symbols. Symbol, for Jung, is an image which a person knows to be of great importance but which cannot be explicitly understood or adequately explained. Symbols are expressions of profound mystery, felt as desire, as goal, as fear. A sign, on the other hand, points to something known, but perhaps slightly out of immediate reach.

Awe comes upon one who experiences the presence of a living symbol, as with my first encounter with the Isenheim Crucifixion. Not all renderings of the cross or the crucifixion have this effect upon me. I am familiar with their message. In contrast, Grünewald's Crucifixion, what he caught in it, and what caught him, has the power Jung associated with symbol. Why Grünewald's painting has such an effect upon me and not another has to do both with the piece as an authentic carrier of archetypal authority and with the psychological situation of the observer. The two must meet for the connection to take hold.

Jung pointed out that psychological research is made difficult by just this subjective factor. No observer can abstract him/herself from what is observed. A subjective process takes place in observation that influences the content of what is seen. One's own connection with one's inner patterning skews the observation. The analysis of a work of art, therefore, is not only a matter of aesthetics and historical perspective. It also may be a matter of living archetypal presence engaging the observer.

Archetypes lead a sovereign life of their own, quite independent of conscious direction, even as the outer world has a similar autonomy vis-à-vis the ego. Archetypes cannot be directly or immediately perceived. They are inferred from underlying repetitive motifs of cognition and behavior and can be noted as universally present within contemporary and historical cultures. One senses an archetypal presence in images that produce personal experiences of strong emotional power. That archetypes exist is a postulation for which Jung amassed evidence over a life-time of investigation.

Archetypes presumably have had their origin in the primal beginning of pattern in animal and human life. They have gained their fundamental place within the psyche through confirming repetition in each ensuing generation. Since our primal beginning–however imagined–was prehistoric, the language of archetype is mythological; our ancestors bequeathed to us a predisposition to tell stories and form images reflexively, so that we might have some inkling of who we are, itself a pattern. James Hillman explains it this way: "Myth is . . . a revelation of the dynamics and processes in the archetypal world. . . . Myths not only tell how humans and God interact but they *are that interaction*."[4]

Jung believed that universal human patterned experiences–such as birth, mothering, fathering, coming together, coming apart, death–left their cumulative and evolutional imprint upon psyche. Archetypes take on personalized form when they appear to an individual in need, desire, and behavior, first and foremost. They are present and expected in every human being and are taken for granted by everyone. Further, they appear in more symbolic form in fantasies and dreams in individuals, in myths and fairy tales in culture. Birth, for example, is clearly an original and personal experience for everyone, yet as pattern it is not novel. The archetype repeats itself in the individual and in the group. Archetypes, as such, are theoretical constructs. But images of archetypes, personifications of patterns, are quite specific to individuals and cultures, appearing as the dramatis personae of every personal or collective story. Story, then, or myth, is the "revelation of the dynamics and processes in the archetypal world,"[5] composed of event, outside, and dream, fantasy, imagination inside, as story emerges in a person's history.

Jung categorized certain types of images that inhabit the universal dimension of the psyche, beneath the surface of a person's ego.

Shadow. Of particular importance to my treatment of the

Isenheim altarpiece are personifications of what Jung called the shadow. Shadow images are archetypal in that they capture a dark pattern that is never absent in human experience. Shadow images are always opposed to ego–threat, disequilibrium, a foreign element, something that needs to be hidden, something about us that we reject in order to maintain stability and self-esteem. For Jung, there can be no functioning ego without shadow as its opposite, its antithesis.

The therapeutic purpose in knowing one's shadow is to complete, flesh-out, and challenge the ego, the personality one is glad to show, the personality that establishes worth. Owning one's shadow is extremely hard work; it cuts through pretension and brings one closer to personal honesty. Shadow is our "other side," furtive, embarrassing, hidden. The bad stuff we reject in us falls into the shadow; we are often unconscious of it and always highly defensive in protection of ego. The gates of recognition are guarded by narcissistic self-regard. Jung considered this to be infantile, since it is natural to the child but an obstruction to the mature personality.

Shadow suggests that ego, our sense of "I," is limited, not the whole story of who I am as a publicly acceptable individual. While I might think well of myself (or think that I think well of myself), to be mature requires me to realize that who I am as "ego" is but a portion of who I am and what I might have been had things gone differently. So, paradoxically, not all aspects of shadow are negative. Due to the necessarily partial character of ego, much of my potential has been left behind in my development. I have made choices and choices were made for me. Ego is bent in one direction or another by conditioning. The psychodynamic value of shadow is not only insistence upon ego-modesty. It also con-

tributes to my larger self-consciousness, increasing my awareness that I project onto others what is foreign to my limited
self-understanding. I come to realize that my personal ego
is but a small part of the human spectrum of possibility,
aspects of which might genuinely belong to a larger view of
myself. I give to others, to carry for me, values and characteristics, both dark and light, that lie nascent within my
personality.

Important as the individual application may be, Jung's
concept of shadow extends far beyond personal psychology,
showing the seriousness of his ethical concern. As one moves
deeper into shadow, one encounters a substratum of evil. Ego
seems self-evidently absolute to us as naively conscious persons, but Jung was a romantic philosopher: he viewed ego
within the larger context of psyche, with its many impersonal
aspects. He postulated shadow as existing quite beyond one's
personal ego needs, as a wellspring pattern in psyche from
which individual shadow springs. Jung's shadow is, archetypally considered, objective Evil. Its rootage plumbs far
deeper in the foundation of psyche than personal darkness,
partiality, self-aggrandizing motivation. As human failure,
shadow might seem to be inevitable, and finally forgivable.
But evil as such is quite a different story.

Evil as ontological reality was a major issue joined in the
early years by theologians and Jung, the focus of strong
disagreement. Today the argument lies largely dormant, probably because it is unresolvable if one approaches the issue from
a conventional theological position. Jung was clear. Psychic
energy is the product of polarization by opposites. Ego is
substantial; it is how we know and experience life. The evil
dimension of shadow, according to Jung, is equally substan-

tial. It is against evil that ego constellates itself. Evil is that from which we turn away in order to protect our image of ego, our fantasy of ego. Yet evil surrounds us and cannot be therapeutized away. The patterns of shadow reach into the core of psyche. Evil is archetypal and everywhere present. The notion of light, of safety, of salvation is meaningless without it.

In the Isenheim Crucifixion painting, evil–shadow–in Jesus is found in his illness and his death. It is also found in the two men who surround him: St. John the Baptist and St. John the Evangelist. The Baptist and the Evangelist carry unrealized aspects of Jesus–they are projections of positive/negative aspects of himself, unlived. The figure of Jesus is always, even in scripture, limited to the boundaries of an individual man. When Jesus is understood as everyman, extended everyman appears in the figures surrounding him. Ordinarily out of sight, the shadow goes everywhere the ego goes and touches the two males with whom he shares the space in the Crucifixion panel.

A caveat. No image can validly be reduced to a "this-means-that" signification. My fantasy draws together the strands of my experience with the Isenheim and works them within a Jungian framework. I run the risk of diminishing both the archetypal energy visited upon me and the painting which inspired it. Certainly I will err, caught in my own limitations as imaginer and as writer. Yet the job cannot be done without introducing the correspondence I see between Jung's categories and Grünewald's figures.

Anima/animus. Beyond the shadow in the unconscious, more out of sight, usually, is another category of figures: contra-sexual opposites to the gender of a person's ego. Jung calls these the anima in a male and the animus in a female. Anima in Latin means soul; animus, spirit. Due to the intensity of gender conditioning, anima and animus are harder than shadow to grasp as belonging to one's personality. For a boy, say, his femininity is more difficult to encompass than is his badness. Femininity is ego-dystonic; badness is not so much, due to the mother problem always faced by young males. Since one ordinarily identifies his or her ego with the gender of body, the contra-sexual aspect of one's personality is obscure and more-or-less hidden from consciousness.

In adulthood, anima and animus are activated interpersonally in projection. Other persons, ordinarily of the opposite sex, become the means of Self-discovery. Intrinsic anima/animus becomes extrinsic lover. The contra-sexual aspects of the personality propel a person toward an outer erotic connection, serving one's need for personal completion—salvation, one might say, through gender expression and participation in an opposite through creative union. Thus seen, anima and animus are the subjective means of drawing attention to one's soul and spirit. They open the ego to an experience of the transpersonal. Anima and animus are the press of one's life that stake a claim for that which is not ego. Outer erotic drive is a mirror image of the inner process of individuation.

In scripture, Maria Magdalena is the primary woman in Jesus' life, a sensuous woman, bereft in the loss of her man. Grünewald paints her as the projected image of Jesus' anima. The scriptural account of Jesus' intense inner life, his advocacy of the Kingdom of God as within one, makes plausible the presence of such a woman in his life. As the external projection of Jesus' femininity, Magdalena becomes a representation of his soul, his recessive, potential femininity. Grünewald, who could have painted Christ as a solitary figure upon the cross, surrounded him with men and women who appear on his canvas as expressions of his hidden nature.

Parental imagos. This term was used by Jung when he wrote of the pattern of Mother and Father as precursors of life. At a deep place in the collective unconscious, probably below the shadow and the anima/animus, are remnants, metaphors, equivalencies, amplifications, tones, senses of parental figures. The parental imagos function as forebearers, nurturers, protectors, providers of strain, to which families, clans, religions, and political movements testify. The parental imagos, according to Jung, "are generated subjectively . . . [they] do not arise out of the actual personal experiences of the parents . . . but are based . . . on the activities of the archetypes."[6] As physical parents precondition ordinary life, so the parental imagos as archetypes dominate ordinary psyche; they predispose animal patterns of parenting and instinctual parenting expectation. Parenting belongs to the primordial myth of beginning.

Human mothers and fathers are joined together on an animal level by inherited patterns expressed as and in erotic desire and community need. Instinctual sexual pressure and offspring protection are determined by archetypal parental imagos which human beings inherit and experience. But here again there is more, and once again, the more, psychologically, is Jung. Human beings import meaning to instinctual requirement.

In the Isenheim Crucifixion, the Mother is brilliantly white, starkly and explicitly important. She stands to the side of her son in rigid correspondence with the rocky surrounding terrain. There is no apparent Father image in the panel, as there might have been in a classically medieval painting of the crucifixion, reigning above and beyond in the distance. There is no space for the Father between the horizontal timber of the cross and the upper frame of the painting. The sky is a black background, a vast emptiness between the cross and the earth line.

The Self. English speakers have difficulty getting a handle on Jung's concept of the Self, probably his most perplexing notion. We use the word as a reflexive pronoun referring to what Jung called the ego. His use of Self as a noun standing alone has the ego as small and the Self as great, transpersonal, supraordinate. To grasp his meaning requires one to imagine who or what it is that we speak to when we talk to our "self," when "self" is something other than ego. And then to go beyond that self to Self, understanding its authority as that of The Great Man/Woman Within. The Self is not an introject, as is Freud's superego—once outside, now inside—however much its voice may be colored by one's environment. Nor is it the voice of a complex. It is the archetype of structure, cohesion, and intentionality in psyche, often, although not always, personified.

Jung's Self is the context within which subsidiary personifications—the shadow, the anima/animus, and the parental imagos—find their core. The Self is the vortex of psyche, ". . . a circle whose center is everywhere and circumference is nowhere."[7] It is the central organizing ground of psychic reality and also, paradoxically, its outer totality. Even more paradoxically, the Self is utterly personal, even intimate, if one permits oneself to think such a thing. One has no awareness of the Self until a way is found to move beyond the ego to a supernatural dimension of the psyche. It is with the concept of the Self that Jung returned to the religious background from which he withdrew in his early adult years.

C. A. Meier, Jung's early student, wrote that

> Jung empirically discovered [that] 1. The human psyche has an autochthonous (natural) religious function [and that] 2. No patient in the second half of life has been cured without that patient's finding an approach to his religious function.[8]

The Self cannot be equated with what religious believers call God, but psychologically it functions in a similar way. Jung held that pictures human beings identify as God are, psychologically considered, god-*images*, which may or may not coincide with a theological God. God-images have emotional importance because they are psychological phenomena. The presence of Self in the psyche makes an experience of transcendence possible. In *Aion*, Jung wrote that the Self ". . . can appear in all shapes from the highest to the lowest, inasmuch as these transcend the scope of the ego personality in the manner of a daimonion."[9]

The Self appears as a superior presence, royalty, great man or woman, historical personage, revered relative, exceptionally ugly person, child, animal, bird, insect, flower, mountain, lake. In its most abstract form, the Self takes a geometric pattern, a circle or square with a specific center, a mandala. To be authentic, it must be experienced by a person with a degree of numinosity, awe, *tremendum*, terror, respect. A manifestation of the Self awakens one's capacity to bridge the gap between polarities in the psyche, most importantly between ego and divinity.

Jung interpreted Christ psychologically as a collective symbol of the Self in the Christianized world. He did not mean by this that the Christ figure *is* the Self, but that it functioned as an outer–cultural–manifestation of an inner cultural cohesion. Whether Christ today is a Self-symbol for an individual depends upon his/her personal inner perception. Of this there can be little doubt: as a collective representation, Christ today is more sign than symbol. The image is familiar and collectively exhausted by two millennia of use.

ON SEEING ARCHETYPALLY

On a 1991 visit to Colmar, I entered the Underlinden and encountered the Crucifixion for perhaps the tenth time. I sat again on the bench before it for half an hour, emptying myself, absorbing. I saw something I had not noticed before. The cross on which Jesus is nailed changes planes. At the top, the "I" beam is turned slightly to the viewer's left. Somewhere behind the body, perhaps at the groin, the wood turns, so that behind Jesus' legs it is turned slightly to the right. I have no notion of why Grünewald might have twisted the cross in such a way.

Similarly, archetypal psychology enables a double plane of vision. On one plane, I see a figure from a religious story, familiar to everyone. On another plane, what I see does not connect me with a story but with brokenness, sordidness, pain. On a literal plane, I have no experience with crucifixion. On the other plane, what I here call an archetypal dimension, collecting the shards of my own patterns of brokenness into an emotional response, crucifixion is a metaphorical way of understanding what I myself have known. Crucifixion is a way of imaging my experience of being broken, outcast, humiliated, overcome. My connecting image with experience and emotion produces the awe that Jung claimed was always present when the archetypal Self moves into focus.

My brokenness collapses my spirit, diminishes my confidence, foretells the end of life as I want it. Understood as archetype, brokenness takes on new meaning; it is no longer only an individual peculiarity, something I might go into therapy to correct. As I go into the ground of my abyss, the "I" beam angles in a different direction. Then, when I gaze upon the Crucifixion, I am in touch with a universal aspect of the terror I feel at a fore-vision of my own end. In Edward Casey's words, "The image is not *what* is present to awareness—this is the content proper—but *how* this content is presented."[10]

And so I sit before the Isenheim experiencing the archetype in the image crossing over the archetype in myself. My feeling is the elaboration of the archetype.

In the 1991 film *The Object of Beauty*, a deaf and dumb chambermaid in an elegant London hotel steals a small Henry Moore male bust from a bedroom. The poor maid is unaware of the dollar value of the piece; she took it because "he spoke to me," being totally aware of its value to her as an archetypal image. She was the only person in the film so aware. Jung's archetypal notion provides a basis for seeing at the Underlinden what the chambermaid heard coming from the statuette.

What one sees is psyche, the twist in the plane of Grünewald's cross.

4

THE QUESTION OF DISEASE IN THE CRUCIFIXION PANEL

> The model for the Christ crucified is the festering corpse
> of one pitifully wracked with frightful disease. The altar
> was painted for the monastery of St. Anthony at which
> venereal diseases were treated, and the artist has taken
> such a broken and diseased body as might have been
> seen there to symbolize the agony of the Redemption.
>   David Robb and J. J. Garrison,
>   *Art in the Western World*

ILLNESS

THE FIRST, AND LASTING, IMPACT MADE UPON ME BY THE
Isenheim Crucifixion was the impression of illness, underlined
by Jesus' enormous presence, twice the size of the other figures
in the panel. His body is strongly masculine, well muscled
and proportioned, in spite of its emaciation. His skin is
greenish, the color of putrefaction, and covered with bumps,
pustules, outbreakings. The sores have a leaden color, suggesting an inner poison rising to the surface. His hands and
feet are deformed, contorted, and swollen.

The scriptural accounts of the passion mention Jesus' having been beaten, and it is, of course, plausible to interpret
the skin eruptions on the Isenheim Christ as the result of
brutal treatment. Pieces of wood, present in the painting in
some of the lesions, may have dislodged from branches and

stuck in the skin of a man undergoing a thrashing. These tiny pieces of wood repeat the ignominy of the crown of thorns on Jesus' head.

Yet there is more. In the Entombment panel, just below the Crucifixion, the suggestion of illness is even more pronounced. Christ's skin is yellowish, perhaps jaundiced. The sores are more frankly lesions, open, as though running, and fresh blood is seen. It is my impression that a rash or infection is present – an illness coming from the inside out rather than an injury imposed from the outside. The Entombment wounds look like eruptions. The thorns are gone. One sees morbid changes in the structure of the skin.

In the Temptation of St. Anthony panel of the altarpiece, a small, gnome-like man crouches in the lower-left corner. In his ulcerous body there can be no doubt of illness. Large scabs and festering lumps cover his body. His face, stomach, and lower legs are inflamed. His hands and feet are not just deformed, as in the Crucifixion. Where his left hand was is a stump, and his right foot is deviate, having moved away from a human toward an animal form. Grünewald let his imagination run riot in this panel. The creatures attacking St. Anthony are clearly allegorical, fantastic beasts behaving like humans, or humans in the likeness of beasts: explicit degradation. The only figure who is recognizably human is the gnome at the bottom, closest to the viewer. He disintegrates: wracked with pain, demented, distended with infection, regressing to a primitive state. He clutches Anthony's breviary with the remnants of a hand that is all rot and decay.

The gnome, the Entombment, and the Crucifixion share a common motif. Grünewald painted three pictures of a com-

mon disease suffered by the men who found their way to the
Isenheim hospice: less severe in Christ, more diabolical in the
gnome. This impression is supported by Hayum, who wrote,
". . . there is no question . . . that the Altarpiece's imagery
has been shaped by the particular context . . . around the
themes of disease and healing."[1] Hayum certainly had the
three figures I mention in mind.

There was a stipulation in the 1477(8?) Reforms of the Antonian order concerning the reception of patients: *"le lendemain doit être admené devant la crotte[2] dudit hôpital et visité pour
savoir si la maladie est du feu infernal. . . ."*[3] To name the disease
feu infernal was not to specify it. This was a blanket categoriza-
tion, dating at least from the ninth century and continuing
through the time of the painting of the Isenheim. The point
is that Grünewald, according to Hayum,

> chooses to transcribe a presumably predetermined program
> [the scriptural story] into a visual language that touches the
> one experienced by these patients. . . . [this] . . . brings out
> . . . dramatically . . . his extraordinary capacity to be affected
> by this context and his evident need to communicate with
> this special group of viewers.[4]

Grünewald may not have wished, or did not dare, to paint
the Crucifixion Christ with all of the symptoms of *feu infernal.* To have done so would have produced a Christ so bizarre
that it would invite rejection. Instead, he may have spread
the symptoms around so that the altarpiece as a whole provided a point of connection for nearly anyone at the Isenheim
hospice. Frank Bové writes in *The Story of Ergot*, "The . . .

Isenheimer Altar . . . portrays . . . victims of St. Anthony's
Fire . . . majestically . . . powerfully."[5] Though Bové does
not mention the Christ figure as one of the victims, I assume
that he intends to include it since only the Crucifixion, the
Entombment, and the gnome in the Temptation of St. Anthony panel lend themselves to such an interpretation.

The Isenheim inmates could have had little hope for a
medical solution. They were nursed, probably not cured.
Psychological healing, however, was another matter, as it continues to be today in illness. By connecting their suffering
to Christ's suffering, a transformation of attitude could begin.
Grünewald's Crucifixion could become a means of relief rather
than condemnation and despair. Their illness was visible in
the image of God. I assume that the patients as well as the
Antonian monks used the chapel at Isenheim. The Antonian reforms of 1477, according to Hayum, "advocate prayer
and entry into the church as a steady routine for patients."[6]

ERGOT

What might have been the disease which brought men
to Isenheim? In the opinion of scholars and medical histor-
ians, it was known in France as *feu infernal* (fire of hell), as
Mutterkornkrankheit (mothercorn/grain illness) in Germany,
as *Ignis Sacer* (holy fire) and *Ignis Plaga* (plague), and as St.
Anthony's Fire everywhere the Antonian monks nursed. The
symptoms depicted in the altarpiece went by other names
as well. They include *Kriebelkrankheit* (crawling illness—
especially when a symptom consisted of the feeling of ants

under the skin), *Erysipilas* (red skin), and *Ergotismus*, when the infecting agent was suspected to be ergot. It was often-confused with epilepsy, leprosy, and, as we shall see, syphilis. In Germany alone, some thirty designations have been found.[7]

Occurrences of the *feu infernal* were connected with an unusually wet planting season followed by a hot summer, which produced a black-ish and hard fungus on grains of rye. When the grain was ground into meal and baked into bread, outbreaks of the illness occurred. The disease took two forms: a necrotic type (more common west of the Rhine), in which tissue dies, especially in the extremities, and a convulsive type, prevalent in eastern Europe. Epidemics of illness attributable to spoiled grain raged throughout Europe in the Middle Ages.

According to C. H. Fuchs, the first widespread outbreak took place in Xanten, near Duisburg, Germany, in 857, when people incurred swollen blisters and a rot which caused their limbs to fall off.[8] An epidemic of *Ignis Plaga* swept Paris in 945; from that point on, all of Europe was affected – from Sweden to Spain, from France to Russia. Epidemics were at their height when the Antonian order was founded in the late eleventh century, but were declining in prevalence at the time Grünewald painted. Due to better agricultural knowl-edge and procedures, epidemics died out by the nineteenth century, except for a bizarre recurrence in Pont St. Esprit, France, in 1951. Hundreds of people and animals were affected, suffering from vomiting, prolonged sleeplessness, pains in the throat and stomach, cold sensations in the limbs, and delir-ium. The infected jumped out of windows because they had visions of being engulfed by flames or attacked by wild beasts. The scourge decimated the village. The horrible story of Pont

St. Esprit can be found in John Fuller's *The Day of St. Anthony's Fire*.[9]

The common denominator in all such poisoned grain epidemics was ergot, the *sclerotium* (hard filament) of the fungus *claviceps purpurea*. The fungus was not confined to medieval Europe. Mexicans, as far back as we have knowledge, knew it as Olaliugui, what is now known as Morning Glory, a hallucinogenic drug. Hippocrates prescribed fungused barley flour to stimulate childbirth. In Roman times, Caius Plinius Secundus (23–79 A.D.) (Pliny) reported that "grain crops could be spoiled . . . by bad weather . . . rust . . . burn . . . carbuncle."[10] The Romans celebrated Robigalia in honor of the god Robigus, who guarded the grain fields against blight.

Ergotismus had the following symptoms: "multiple ulcerations of the skin, a severe inner feeling of heat with an unquenchable thirst (with lividness and fever), necrosis (putrefaction) of toes and fingers, blindness, dementia, nervous and mental degeneration and amnesia."[11] We are here involved, as Bové wrote, in the

> . . . game of guessing what the widespread epidemics mentioned in writings of the Middle Ages really were. Were they the pest? The plague? Erysipilas? Anthrax? Typhus? Ergot poisoning? Exanthema? Leprosy? Smallpox? Ergot poisoning—ergotism, bread poisoning—has been mistaken for all of these and more. . . . Why? Because the terminology used in the early Middle Ages was . . . vague. . . . [W]here they used broad terms such as pestilence, fouling of the body, divine fire and morbid condition the translators [from Latin and Greek] sometimes gave interpretations not meant by the author.[12]

In another entry, Bové adds syphilis to this list.[13]

It has been suggested that ergot may well be called "the drug of this [twentieth] century."[14] It is used in childbirth management, migraine prophylaxis and treatment, psychotic disorders, internal medicine, and geriatrics. Albert Hoffman and Arthur Stoll of Basel discovered its use for the expansion of consciousness. They found that ergot is the source of lysergic acid amide – the parent of LSD. Bové states that LSD

> . . . has the power of depersonalizing us so that we become observers of ourselves and our actions while participating in them. . . . [I]t loosens up our intellectual control so that long suppressed and repressed memories emerge to be seen in vivid visual symbols. Abreaction is intense. In the hands of a skillful psychiatrist, lysergide helps patients with anxiety states and obsessional neurosis release their repressed material so that therapy is possible or at least facilitated. If misused, the consequences are too horrible to contemplate.[15]

Rotting limbs, red flesh, dementia, ulcerations, paralysis – all of these are found or suggested in Grünewald's three portrayals of illness in the Isenheim. Moreover, in both the Temptation and Resurrection panels, one can see a parallel to the visions reported by users of LSD – the former representing a "bad trip" and the latter a "good trip." In my own one-time use of LSD, no magnificent visions of light occurred such as Grünewald painted in his Resurrection, but rather a kind of organic inter-relatedness of nature more similar to the quietly coordinated picture of man-animal-vegetation in the St. Paul and St. Anthony panel. LSD verified for me in personal experience the existence of an archetypal foundation in the psyche.

SYPHILIS

In a further stretch of imagination, a case can also be made for designating syphilis as the disease depicted in the Isenheim altarpiece. Syphilis probably was in the amalgam subsumed under *feu infernal*, etc., in the Middle Ages. As a specific disease designation, syphilis sprang from the imagination of Girolamo Fracastoro of Verona, who in 1530 published a poem entitled *Syphilis sive Morbus Gallicus*. It told of Syphilis, a shepherd who tended his flocks in Alcithous, a fictional place supposedly noted by Columbus's sailors on their way to the New World. Syphilis cried out to the Sun-god in anger, "Why do we worship you? Better that we worship our own king who will help us." Syphilis's king accepted his worship, and the Sun-god retaliated by touching the sea and air with a poison bringing a hitherto unknown pestilence. The first victim, quite naturally, was Syphilis himself, who was afflicted with hideous sores, convulsive members, and sleepless nights. In Greek mythology, Syphilus was one of the twelve children of Niobe, the first mortal woman loved by Zeus. Apollo and Artemis, to avenge Niobe's insult upon their mother, Leto, killed Syphilus with arrows, in the Middle Ages a sign of the plague. Fracastoro thus gave the "new" disease an old name.[16]

Before the designation "syphilis" was coined by Fracastoro, it was known as *il mal Francese* by Dürer, who in 1484 (1496?) made a woodcut of a victim, a delicate fellow with pustules on his arms and legs and a very sad look on his face.[17] Erwin

PLATE 1

PLATE 6

PLATE 7

PLATE 1
Detail of Christ from the Resurrection wing

PLATE 2
Detail of John the Evangelist, Maria, and Mary Magdalena from the Crucifixion panel

PLATE 3
Detail of John the Baptist from the Crucifixion panel

PLATE 4
Detail of Christ from the Crucifixion panel

PLATE 5
The Crucifixion panel, flanked by St. Anthony on its right and St. Sebastian on its left and with the Entombment below

PLATE 6
Detail of Christ from the Crucifixion panel

PLATE 7
Detail from the Temptation of St. Anthony wing

PLATE 2

PLATE 4

PLATE 3

Ackerknecht, the medical historian, states that "from the 12th century on, medieval physicians were richly supplied with mercurial recipes against an anomalous group of chronic skin infections, which, from their very names—scabies grossa, variola grossa, grosse verole, scabies mola, böse Blattern, mal Franzoso, were most blatantly syphilitic."[18] J. M. Charcot, Freud's teacher at the Salpêtrière, in his article "Les Syphilitiques dans L'art" diagnosed the illness of the altarpiece and ranged in his speculations from leprosy to syphilis.[19]

According to an old story, syphilis came to Europe from America, having been contracted by Columbus's sailors in Haiti. It was then spread by these sailors in 1495 to the occupants of Naples, who dispersed it to the remainder of the continent. This is highly unlikely. H. E. Sigerist, the Swiss medical historian, amusingly wrote that "Matthew Lang, Cardinal of Gurk and Bishop Coadjutor of Salzburg, was suffering from syphilis like everybody who was anybody at the time."[20] "The time" was the last part of the fifteenth century—before Columbus's sailors, before Grünewald's painting, before Fracastoro's poem. Thomas Parran wrote, "Leprosy and syphilis continued to be assimilated in popular prejudices over a long period."[21] The medieval doctor John of Gaddesdens (1280–1361) wrote:

> . . . those who cohabit with a woman who has had coitus with a leper have a sensation of stabbing between the flesh and the skin, and sometimes a burning in the whole body, and afterwards frigidity and sleeplessness, and, in the face, a sensation of ants running about.[22]

As we have seen, these were also considered to be the

symptoms of St. Anthony's Fire, *Ergotismus, Kriebelkrankheit*, and *Mutterkornkrankheit*. Cecilia Mettler says that

> . . . in the 13th century, fevers, wasting, epilepsy, the itch, the sacred fire, anthrax, and sore eyes were added to *lepra* in the list of contagious diseases. Bernard Gordon was careful to point out that while lepra may arise from *incortu*[23] with a leper, it can also arise from impure contact.[24]

Every disease manifestation accompanied by ulcerations, gangrene, and malformation of the extremities was then considered leprous. *Ignis Sacer*, which we have already seen was associated with times of famine and poor growing seasons, was also classified among the variations of leprosy, being marked, in its worst stage, by similar symptoms, particularly the mutilation or loss of limbs. Since the various designations mentioned above are difficult to differentiate and since many of their symptoms are indistinguishable from those of syphilis, it is improbable that syphilis suddenly broke upon sixteenth-century Europe full-blown from America on Columbus's ships.

Sir Oswald Osler, the English medical theoretician, comments that "syphilis is the great imitator," inasmuch as it resembles forty diseases of the skin, twenty-three mouth disorders, and sixteen pathological conditions of the genitalia. In tertiary syphilis there is a remarkable similarity to *Ergotismus* in cardiovascular, neurological, and ocular abnormalities. Osler says, "know syphilis and the whole of medicine is open to you. It simulates almost every disease known to man."[25]

Charles Butler claims that references to disease in Exodus 34:7, Leviticus 13:10–15 and 46, Deuteronomy 28:27–28,

Isaiah 3:16 f., and Psalm 38 all implicate syphilis. To quote Isaiah:

> Moreover the Lord saith,
> Because the daughters of Zion are haughty,
> And walk with stretched forth necks
> And wanton eyes,
> Walking and mincing as they go,
> And making a tinkling with their feet:
> Therefore the Lord will smite with a scab
> The crown of the head of the daughters of Zion,
> And the Lord will discover their secret parts.

Inflammation of the eyes and "moth-eaten" hair are secondary symptoms of syphilis. It is clear from the prophet's anger that the disease of the women of Jerusalem was a divine punishment for licentiousness. That connection is very old and is deeply lodged within the Judeo-Christian tradition.

There is resistance in our own time to identifying the Isenheim disease as syphilis. I have already mentioned Mollegen's retraction. Pierre Schmitt, then curator of the Unterlinden Museum in Colmar, told me in 1984 quite flatly that "there is no plague, there is no syphilis" in the Isenheim Crucifixion. Dr. Schmitt's own writing on the Isenheim altarpiece, however, defines the Antonian vocation as emerging "in response to the anguished appeals of a stricken humanity suffering under repeated outbreaks of the plague and of syphilis epidemics."[26]

Similarly, Ackerknecht, quoted to the contrary above, stated to me in August 1976, "Jesus is not sick. The Christus is a picture of a dead man. The wounds come from the outside. There is no connection between the gnome in the St. Anthony panel and the Christ." Later in the same interview, upon further questioning, he said, "Christ is ill, but he does not have syphilis. He has *Mutterkornkrankheit.*" A librarian at the Medical History Library of the University of Zürich said, "Oh, no, it could not possibly be!" A Zürich analyst said, "That interpretation is too concrete." In a sermon in St. Andrew's Church in Zürich, I suggested the syphilitic interpretation. Afterwards, a woman came to me and stated what I suspect is the basis for each of these objections: "How could Jesus have contracted syphilis? He was never immoral!"

It is moot whether syphilis or some form of *Ergotismus* was the actual disease suffered by the Isenheim patients and which Grünewald depicted in the altarpiece. The specific labeling of the disease is not essential to my contention that his portrayal shows evil as indigenous to the divine and thus the human experience of soul. It is evident from the confusion of names in the early sixteenth century that no clear line was drawn between illness stemming from sexual behavior and illness resulting from grain poisoning. Or, in our day, drug poisoning. Poison is inextricably woven into life, including the living of instinct—that is the point of this work.

However, the possibility of syphilis as Christ's disease is symbolically telling precisely because of the negative moral judgment placed upon sexuality. The syphilitic micro-organism *treponema pallidum* requires moisture and warmth to survive. It is interesting that the active agent in ergot producing the fungus on the rye grain grew only when an abnormally wet spring was followed by an abnormally hot summer. This description of a growing season can be translated into human instinctual terms. Jung wrote:

Our Christian doctrine is a highly differentiated symbol that expresses the transcendent . . . —the God image and its properties. . . . This comprises practically everything of importance that can be ascertained about the manifestations of the psyche in the field of inner experience, *but it does not include Nature* [emphasis mine], at least not in any recognizable form. Consequently, at every period of Christianity there have been subsidiary currents or undercurrents that have sought to investigate the empirical aspect of Nature not only from the outside but also from the inside.[27]

Nature, of course, includes sexual instinct, and syphilis is transmitted through the activity of sexual instinct. Sexuality has been omitted from the traditional Christian understanding of transcendence. I understand Grünewald to have rectified the omission. It is my fantasy that Grünewald did so by presenting a Christ so deeply identified with the instinctual nature of humanity that he is pulled into death by an evil consequence of loving.

Syphilis, from a psychological point of view, opens the Isenheim Crucifixion to a wider and more radical interpretation than would otherwise be the case. As in the words of Nietzsche,

. . . to calm the imagination of the invalid, so that at least he should not, as hitherto, have to suffer more from thinking about his illness than from the illness itself—that, I think, would be something! It would be a great deal![28]

Nietzsche's plea for a humane understanding of illness is encompassed in Jung's naming of Christ as a symbol of the Self and in Grünewald's painting of a diseased Savior. A diminishment of moral opprobrium is a kind influence.

AIDS

In our day, AIDS is a parallel to the ravage Grünewald painted in his Isenheim Christ. AIDS can have a sexual point of contagion similar to syphilis. Both may be incurable. Both have moral overtones—they are transmitted by disreputable behavior. Both cause uninfected people to shrink away, afraid to touch, afraid to associate. Both ostracize. Both conditions existed before anyone knew what they were or how they were spread. Both hide and gestate in the body long before they are discovered. The various maladies outlined above as disease possibilities suffered by Grünewald's Christ resemble many of the opportunistic illnesses made possible by the HIV. It has been suggested that tertiary syphilis has disappeared from the physician's office and is masquerading as AIDS.

In *AIDS and Its Metaphors*, Susan Sontag mentions syphilis and leprosy in the same breath as AIDS, not only because of the similarity of symptomatology and incubation, but, even more importantly, because of the scourge-like implications of the illness and the moral degradation attached to it by public opinion. Sontag writes of metaphor because AIDS is understood generally as a punishment for a condition of life, whether this be homosexuality or the poverty that leads to drug addiction. Infected persons become pariahs, and the illness is feared in an apocalyptic sense, as a plague that may engulf the world. The illness becomes an opportunity for blame, for scapegoating, for psychological projection.

For the HIV-positive person, there is presently no cure, only, with a treatment and an attitude that works, postponement. The common thread that binds advanced syphilis and AIDS is twofold: a mortality flashed on the screen of one's awareness, coupled with a common point of contagion – the victim's supposedly unclean life.

Sontag has been free of the symptoms of cancer for a decade. She extends her optimism toward scientific medicine to the AIDS epidemic. But Sontag's own cure – as with everyone – only delays the inevitable. A strong belief in the sufficiency of physical cure encourages the illusion that life can be insulated from the ravages of evil. Terror abounds when terminal illness is in focus, and terror encourages the denial of transience.

Once one becomes HIV-positive, there is little one can do to prevent the inevitable diminishment of T-cells indicating the collapse of the immune system. Malevolence has fixed its hold, disfiguring the life that remains. One is caught in a trajectory with but one outcome. AIDS is a diabolical exemplification of Jung's notion of the substantiality of evil. Whether one blames the sick person or the community that condemns, as Sontag does, one avoids a focus on evil as an unavoidable and necessary ingredient of life. The chimera of a universe that is essentially only good – if one can find the magic bullet – presses the responsibility for evil onto an imperfect humanity. What Sontag does is shift the blame.

The perfectionistic illusion then passes over onto a science which will be able, given time, to cure, to eliminate the evil. Science becomes the "all good," in modern times taking the place of a perfect God. If the issue is responsibility and the tactic is blame, and one removes it from the victim of AIDS, the evil knight on the chess board is bound to move to another square, in this case, collective opinion. The desire to escape personal guilt by placing blame elsewhere becomes a preoccupation that is built upon a false understanding of the psyche. One error that results is the transfer of responsibility onto those whose metaphorical system is different from one's own. All the while, the problem remains: how to understand disease and death as inevitable in the process of living. An example of the pervasive implication of personal wrongdoing was the testimony before Congress, shortly before her death, of Kimberly Bergalis, the young woman who apparently contracted the HIV from a dentist in Florida. Legislation was being considered to test medical professionals for the virus. "I did nothing wrong," she said, "yet I'm made to suffer like this."[29]

Leaving for a later chapter the issue of sexuality as the accomplice in both syphilis and AIDS, I wish to reiterate my primary hypothesis regarding the Isenheim Crucifixion, as it applies to AIDS. Grünewald painted Christ with an illness emerging from inside his body—an endogenous condition rather than a flagrant imposition. Nothing is ever wholly inside or outside, of course. In every duality, each involves something of its opposite polarity. While the HIV does at some point enter one's bloodstream, it subsequently lives and extends itself as a hidden inner enemy. It is passed on from one "within" to another "within." I focus upon this intrinsically interior quality.

The virus is a condition of modern life, a modern example of evil's ubiquitous presence. Christ's suffering was not the fault of the Roman soldiers or governors, nor the fault of the Jews. Nor is it the fault of contemporary men and women, whatever their sexual behavior or manner of drug use. Evil abounds, whether it is neurotic, or imposed by the strong against the weak, or comes as a bolt from the blue to one who has crossed every "t" and dotted every "i." Suffering is a condition of life because evil is a condition of life. One can only deny evil; one cannot avoid it.

I write here about the presence in our lives of the virus, not about the responsibility everyone has both to avoid infection and avoid passing it on. But once one is contagious, involved personally in the inexorable illness, Grünewald's crucified Christ might be seen as I imagine the Isenheim patients might have seen that stark image dominating their chapel: a revolutionary picture of psychological reality quite aside from one's faith in a particular religious system. Moralizing about sexual preference and behavior becomes irrelevant; the issue is sickness and death. Even the gods get sick and die, as the Isenheim Crucifixion demonstrates.

5

CHRIST AND EVIL

... the Christian image of the [S]elf—Christ—lacks the shadow that properly belongs to it.

C. G. Jung,
CW 9, ii, § 79

If you look into the eyes of someone with AIDS you can see the face of God.

Mark Dyer
Bishop of Bethlehem, PA

MORAL PARADOX

I APPROACH GRÜNEWALD'S STRANGE, DARK CHRIST BY WAY of moral paradox, found in the interlacing network of good and evil in the core of the psyche. I say strange because neither Christian doctrine nor secular culture, rooted in its Christian past, has prepared me to see evil in Christ. The notion frightens me, the more so as I allow myself to imagine the ramifications of a Christ who carries all of reality within himself as intrinsic.

Often I feel a resistance within me that impedes my ability to let the words within me come forth. Then I can understand Jung's fear as a child when he had the unthinkable thought of God defecating on the Basel cathedral—I am in touch with my own childish and childlike fears.[1] Since I am a Jungian analyst, talk of "the integration of ego and shadow" rolls off my tongue with alacrity, but it is not so easy for me to let the impact of moral paradox as a condition of transcendence-in-life sink into my heart. I continue to gasp at horrors in the news as though they were elements foreign to life.

Darkness and light coexist in psyche, since they are universally present in human experience. And if it is so that psyche is home for imagination, that psyche is the fundament of reality, then it must also be so that the image of Christ as an abundant focus for psyche's center must contain darkness and light as well.

For example, the human experience of peace is necessarily preceded by turmoil, without which peace has no reference point. Taken to their highest—and lowest—power, both peace and turmoil are experiences also of the transpersonal or holy; in short, they are sacred emotions. Relief comes to human beings after, and not without, an experience of anguish. By the same token, claiming that the Christ figure is a symbol of the Self and is thus a manifestation of psyche's center, as did Jung, can be supported only when Christ is understood as representing both light and shadow.

The idea is not new in Christian tradition, however much it is obscure. In I Corinthians 1:13, 20, 25, Paul wrote:

Is Christ divided? . . .

. . . hath not God made foolish the wisdom of this world?

. . . the foolishness of God is wiser than men; and the weakness of God is stronger than men.

In speaking of God, Paul uses foolishness and weakness as

descriptions. I have heard and read those sentences a thousand times in forty years of ministry without quite knowing what I heard. Did I think that Paul meant that the notion of a foolish God was so absurd that it put to rest any pretensions of human wisdom? Probably. Yet approached the other way around, taking his words as more than a figure of speech, Paul is stating that indeed Christ is both weak and strong—in my words, dark and light. The unity of God as containing human disparates confounds rationality, since rationality is pervasively linear and logical, unable to contain paradox. Wisdom and foolishness are opposites, as are light and darkness; presumably they cannot exist together in the same form. Yet, according to Paul, wisdom does not exclude foolishness as an attribute of Christ as the image of God. Paul provides a scriptural basis for moral paradox.

Jung's conjoining of good and evil in psyche need pose no insurmountable barrier for Christians. If God can be foolish and weak and simultaneously wise and strong, then God holds together good and evil, for foolishness and weakness are part of evil, as we know evil. Paul joined the opposites together in his teaching about Christ, the unifying image. The church confirmed Paul's teaching in the Nicene Creed, ". . . God . . . maker of heaven and earth, of *all* that is, seen and unseen" (emphasis mine).

In this chapter, I consider Jung's concept of shadow not as personal darkness, but as intrinsic to being, ontological. As such, evil is fundamental to psyche and in the unconscious, psyche's hidden half. Jung saw ontological evil as absolute and inextricable, a necessary opposite to good. He called it substantial, a far different understanding than that of scholastic theology, from which Western understandings have grown. To Jung, evil was not the absence or diminishment of essential goodness. It was pervasive, ineluctable, co-essential. Evil led into good and away from it, as "blackness is the beginning of whiteness."[2]

Following Jung, it is impossible to reduce profound evil to incomplete good, no matter how deeply one might feel the need to protect good as a desired moral principle. To do so depreciates the strain present in all genuine conflict; it invites the chimera of escape from the often unbearable tension that good and evil ground together leave in their wake. Absolute evil is the abyss, the nightmare, that Western humanity feels as its darkest fear and apprehension, the apocalypse from which there is no escape, the tunnel which has no light at its end. Primo Levi knew this, after his release from Auschwitz in 1945:

> . . . this is the awful privilege of our generation and of my people, [that] no one better than us has ever been able to grasp the incurable nature of the offense, that spreads like a contagion. It is foolish to think that human justice can eradicate it. It is an inexhaustible fount of evil; it breaks the body and spirit of the submerged, it stifles them and renders them abject; it returns as ignominy upon the oppressors, . . . and swarms around in a thousand ways, against the very will of all, as a thirst for revenge, as a moral capitulation, as denial, as weariness, as renunciation.[3]

> . . . it was a naive hope, like all those that rest on too sharp a divison between good and evil. . . .[4]

Levi died by his own hand in 1987.

The 259 human beings who went down with Pan Am Flight 103, on 21 December 1988 at Lockerbie, Scotland, and the eleven persons in its path on the ground met absolute evil as a fate. Mystery abounds in destiny falling upon one particular flight on one particular path over Scotland. The mystery will never be resolved by the determination of personal responsibility and subsequent guilt, whether the emphasis be more rationally placed upon the perpetrators and/or the careless or, irrationally, upon the part of the dead, whose karma supposedly directed them to embark on Pan Am 103. The people on board and on the ground encountered a vein of malignancy that lurks everywhere in life, "blowing where it listeth." It could be called the dark side of the Holy Spirit.

Knowing shadow as ontological evil is essential to psychological understanding. Conversely, believing that life can be without shadow is illusory, Jung's great point. The chimera of perfection, splitting good and evil, with evil a transgression, as spoken of by Levi, underwritten by an essence that is only good, is a fond, baseless hope. We are forced to wage war against some evil or another that is always an enemy, always defeatable, if only the correct blame were to be found. We compulsively defend and devastate, spending our lives ferreting out responsibility, miserable because something might be left undone that might have prevented a bad happening. We slosh about in naivete, trapped in an endless cycle of searching out the perpetrator, seeking an existence impervious to inexplicable disaster. As the wife of a 103 passenger said: "It is a great mystery, all this evil. I don't really understand it."[5]

The Pan Am 103 disaster is complicated by the United States Navy's destruction of an Iran Air flight over the Persian Gulf in July 1988, killing 290 people. That ignominious event was first denied as its responsibility by the United States and then admitted, but with weak explanation and even weaker apology. Killing civilians, whether by error or intention, is an inescapable implication of a sensibility unburdened by moral paradox. We are good and the enemy is evil, and good has a right that evil does not have. The result is a civilization shored up by technological prowess and stealth, by pretensions of righteousness. Evil is the more enhanced by protestations of innocence; the obligation to pretend that we are what we say we are stands over us like a sledgehammer. It is so pervasive that, even as I write about paradox, I become aware that I am entangled in assigning gradations of culpability.

According to David Miller, Professor of Religion at Syracuse University, a memorial was dedicated there to the Syracuse students who were aboard Pan Am 103. A number of parents objected to the use of the word "tragedy" describing the crash; university officials agreed to replace the stone, using, instead, "bomb." I respect the tenacity with which the survivors of the passengers on 103 have pursued the case through seemingly endless international bureaucratic obfuscation, hard after fact, responsibility, and reform. The memorial controversy, however, illustrates my point in using Flight 103 as an example. Tragedy is a condition of life, an inescapable ingredient in moral paradox. The students, intent upon education and Christmas family celebration, walked unknowingly into their downfall. "Bomb" connotes only evil intent by the terrorists.

As I use the word, "perfection" expresses our yearning for an existence beyond, and simultaneously short of, paradox and the ensuing conflict that appears whenever the variations

III

of good and evil clash. Perfection's hold on us leads us to expect a flight across the ocean without worry of terrorism, metal fatigue, or error-prone pilots. Passengers rely upon the law of averages, telling themselves not to worry. Beneath this need to feel safe, the two martinis, and the ominous silence on takeoff is a terror of catastrophe, a threat of lurking evil with which the ego must deal. Just when we begin to believe there is no real danger, to trust the advertising, another vein erupts. Aviation and medicine are contemporary paradigms for our desire to live without the complexity of moral paradox; extraordinary advances have been made in both fields by scientific research and development. We seize upon encouragement. But the illusion does not hold. Evil insists upon asserting itself.

In Zürich in 1991, I visited a small park behind the main train station where narcotics were openly and legally sold and used. In the midst of a city sparkling with every desirable urban amenity was a scene of human degradation unparalleled in my experience. I sat on a rock near—but not too near—the circular bazaar of dope. A young man with a new purchase, preparing to shoot up, sat nearby and spoke: "Do you like what you see? It's the game of life. And for many of us it will soon be over."

To obey my impulse to turn away from that scene would have been a turning away from the Grünewald Crucifixion. I ask even now: what I must do is get this darkness into my system, to know that the Zürich marketplace with its suffering is the motif of the Grünewald Crucifixion? Grünewald's Christ, the Self, the transcendent, whatever I call it, is in the bloody gauzes underfoot, the arms so blackened and scarred that a needle will not enter, in the stuporous bodies, many in almost catatonic postures of worship, surrounding me. The Zürich park is revelation, the place of the dark Christ. My knowing the Self in my personal anguish is gnosis. My knowing the Self in the Zürich cesspool is mystical.

I struggled out of the park, slightly deranged, unfit to talk to my wife waiting for me in the station. I was caught in the madness of crucifixion, impaled upon a conventional mind.

Jung wrote in *Aion* that "the idea of good and evil . . . are [*sic*] a logically equivalent pair of opposites and, as such, the *sine qua non* of all acts of cognition. . . . good and evil . . . do not derive from one another but are always there together."[6] I might read those words at a distance from Zürich's needle park on a train to the mountains and reflect, "Nice point; Jung's really got something there. Makes a lot of sense." Would I say the same were my son or daughter in that park, or on Flight 103, or if I found that I were HIV positive? I retreat. I sit on my vine-covered loggia overlooking the lake in Ascona, mini-bar handy, and celebrate life. I think that I am in harmony with the universe.

I am enmeshed in the illusion. My conditioning regarding good and evil is insidious. I slip off the razor's edge of moral paradox. Evil, then, becomes not the substantial half of life that it is, but the result of wrong-minded kids, corrupt dope peddlers, stupid city-fathering. Something needs to be corrected. Or, I need to get away from whatever evil influence impinges upon me, to leave the city, to get a divorce, to tie a yellow ribbon round the old oak tree. Debate about personal or collective responsibility for evil serves to obscure. The blame we fix turns out to be a modest accomplishment compared to the nuance, the sense of meaning in anguish, buried under chimeric avoidance.

MYSTERY

But we speak the wisdom of God in a mystery. . . .

I Corinthians 2:7

Moral paradox opens a door to the awareness of mystery and soul. Poetry, mythology, implication, metaphor, and image come to our aid. There is no other aid. I am reminded, once again, of my friend Peter Grey (see chapter one), who exclaimed over and over in his enthusiasm at St. Clement's, "The Mystery! The Mystery! This is a place of the Mystery!" He was the only person, then, to say that sort of thing, and he did so out of an abstruse literary background which I could not, and still do not, altogether comprehend. At the same time, I knew that he spoke for me and for others who came to that intensely sacramental place with no vocabulary to speak of the potent mix of myth and politic taking place there in the sixties. At its best, St. Clement's was an amalgam of the spiritually and culturally dispossessed who found a stage that celebrated their standing on the edge.

Mystery and symbol. A mystic is aware of symbol as a known semblance of the unknown. It is one thing to know what one is doing and to go about it with deliberation. It is quite another thing to know and do, simultaneously sensing that knowing and doing are pieces of a larger quantum that is beyond intentionality. I am not a mystic. I am an extravert—one who is drawn by the "outside," whose energy is primarily galvanized by external objects. Extraverts are never, in the deepest fiber of their being, mystics. But extraverts can know something of the unknown, that emptiness where mystics live. Extraverts can know that appearance is but appearance, even when energy is attached to the appearance. The interior world may be blurred and semi-real, but it is there.

Mystery emerges for everyone, even extraverts, in symbol. For me, mystery is present when I reach a limit to what I can think and I am inched into a space where a different kind of knowledge – a non-knowledge knowledge – becomes almost tactile. I am so accustomed to knowing where I am and what I am doing that when I am elsewhere I am surprised. Genuine mystics are never really surprised. They know the interstices. They expect to live life as symbol.

Seeds of mystery are present in the most common of cognitive acts. On my sabbatical in Zürich, I was alone for two months before my wife came. I was silent for days at a time, often sitting in my sixth-story study staring at a grove of spruce trees, whose tops were slightly above my line of sight. Blackbirds flew in and out of the branches. One would land, weighing down an already drooping branch. I wondered: why did that bird choose that branch, and why, then, did it move from a lower to a higher branch? Or I looked up just at a moment of landing. I might never have looked up, never hesitated from my task long enough to see. I knew what I was seeing on an extraverted basis: blackbirds flying in and out of trees. I didn't know what I was seeing on a mystical basis, but I did know that I was seeing it.

Moments of seeing and wondering are human gateways into mystery. When I ponder I stroke my soul. Extraversion obscures the pleasure of soul stroking. Surprise may not even occur. And soul sinks into a non-experienced oblivion, ready, possibly, but unawakened.

Common stuff indeed, hardly out of the reach of anyone. No great conclusions might be reached from birds and trees, and none need be. Some ordinary ones come only much later, when, say, I get a sense of missing a moment of awareness, in a liminal time of musing with myself. Sometimes when I awake early in the morning in Pennsylvania and sit in my kitchen waiting for the water to boil, I look out at that borderline time of day, when darkness and light mix together. I am pulled into an almost unknown part of myself, an unfamiliar secret place which all but disappears when the activities of the morning begin.

The doctrine of the Incarnation in Christianity is my favorite. It expresses the mystical importance of the ordinary, like birds in trees. In the Incarnation, the visible and invisible, the spiritual and the corporeal, are joined together in the image of Christ. In the Incarnation, the invisible becomes visible in the flesh of Jesus as Christ. It establishes the principle that common flesh, the human form, contains within itself, as Urperson, the grand unseen design of God.

Grünewald's Crucifixion adds a remarkable extension to the Incarnation that is missing in orthodox Christian tradition. Grünewald painted a sick Christ, sick unto death, embellishing the doctrine's teaching that Christ is body as well as spirit by including an incorporation of experienced evil as well as good within his image. Grünewald's Crucifixion presents a more encompassing human picture than orthodoxy provides in its emphasis upon an image of good beset by exogamous evil. It is a vast and novel expansion of opposites contained in a Christ figure.

The expansion could not have been done without a portrayal of a darkness that is inherent in mystery. The thought structures of modern Western-style societies, dominated by patriarchy's rational denial of the unconscious, hold darkness at bay as an enemy, an intrusive, extraneous stranger. Darkness is non-being, lostness, disorientation, ignorance. Darkness is alien, akin to the mindless force of nature, linked to the earth and hidden beneath it, impeding the human struggle for survival. Darkness is the condition of prenatal origin, when the fetus sleeps in powerless pre-consciousness. Darkness is the grave, the depths of the sea, oblivion. Darkness's closeness to mystery pits mystery against enlightenment.

I. M. Lewis, an anthropologist at the London School of Economics, wrote in *Ecstatic Religion* about shamanistic possession:

> . . . [it] asserts the supremacy of the gods as the arbiters of both disorder and order since both are their gift. . . . The transcendental mystery which lies at the heart of [the shaman's] vocation is the healer's passion; his ultimate triumph over the chaotic experience of raw power which threatened to drag him under.[7]

The chaos of raw power, threatening to drag the shaman under, is the terror of every ego, focused here in the healer's initiation. Lewis knows and respects psychoanalytic literature. He connects with crude nature, acknowledging Freud; he connects with transcendent mystery, acknowledging Jung. The power of unchecked, violent nature, whether it rises from the depths or descends from the skies, is the tornado that in an instant tore my cousin's house from over his head in

Minnesota, the catastrophic fire that consumed another cousin's house in Oakland, almost before she could get out of the shower. It is the psychotic rage in which a friend's daughter ripped in half a steel putty knife. It is Pan Am 103.

In "the raw power of nature which threatened to drag him under," the shaman faces this same omnipresent evil. To survive, to gain his authority, the shaman must draw evil power into himself and contain it. He must take into himself that which he fears – the heart of the mystery. In the Isenheim Crucifixion, chaos is implicit in the festering pustules, the outcropping of poison, the lesions portending decay in the body. Grünewald painted Christ consumed by a pathology that is endemic to existence, cosmic in its pervasiveness, vortexed into a single, shamanistic figure. The secret revealed is the same as that which the healer must endure: enlighten-ment-through-darkness. Out of this same chaotic experience comes the Isenheim Resurrection panel, hidden within the altarpiece. Grünewald entered the abyss in the Crucifixion; the Resurrection is its fiery, polar antithesis.

Drawing power from evil seems a strange undertaking for Christ, and indeed it is, if one understands Christ as only the symbol of light in a bifurcated psyche. But moral paradox might be grasped at this point in large measure and in small. Jesus' lonely times, at the beginning of his ministry when he came into direct contact with temptation, at the end in Gethsemane, were invasions from the chaotic unconscious. In his isolation, he heard "another voice," at odds with his sense of himself, at odds with his religious tradition of a dependable father god. Scripture names the antagonistic voice Satan; Jesus puts it behind him; he refuses to allow it to lead him. But wherever, before or behind, Satan is present and Jesus must drink of his cup. In his aloneness, when inner edges rear up to be crossed, Jesus gives the devil his due and allows the gulf to overwhelm. He emerges from his solitariness able to be forsaken. He engages the power of evil not on ego's terms, but as one who knows the source of ambivalence.

Grünewald would long since have taken his place amongst competent painters had he been simply obedient to convention and excellent in his craft. How did he come upon his power-laden seam of originality? Did Grünewald himself borrow from evil? I wonder about that as I sit, afraid and frozen before my typewriter, my mind refusing to work, my fingers refusing to work his dark Christ. Did Grünewald think the unthinkable thought? Did his mind also refuse to stretch Christ into a figure revealing evil? Did his fingers stop, rebelling? Did he press on anyway, into his own version of the void?

As I strain to put my Grünewald imagination into words, I determine not to smoke. I must be able to write about evil in God without reaching for a cigarette to break the impasse. I pace the floor, I chew packages of Nicorette, I tell myself, "I do not smoke." I call upon my higher power. I meditate, I swim, I eat carrots, I have loving connections with my wife, I remember my emphysemic father. And then, with guilt and anticipation and relief, I am at the counter with my money— and I am able to think unthinkable thoughts again. Giving in to addiction is, of course, mis-obedience. But in a way it is not. The struggle to put the forbidden into words does not lessen. Evil is present with me even as I write about evil and I take, I borrow, from it. In my tiny way, I incarnate the good and evil conjunction I seek to convey.

URPERSON AND SALVATION

Anthropos is the Greek word meaning man, or mankind. It is the traditional word used in mythological literature for the imaginary primordial human being, the archetype of the original human figure. But the word "anthropos" is a classical example of the way patriarchal language is based upon a singularly masculine imagery; it can no longer be used as once it was. My assistant, Alice Petersen, coined a new word in German, *Urperson* (pronounced oor-per-sohn), to replace anthropos. As far as we know, there is no such German word. *Ur* means original or primordial; *person*, as in English, spans the gender issue. Urperson, as anthropos, is the mythological basis of the biblical image of the First Adam, the prototype of Christ, and the Second Adam, Jesus as the Christ, presented in the New Testament.

Jung believed that consciousness requires a separation of an original unity into subject and object. Without subject/object separation, externality remains a function of subjectivity: the outer world is projection. And subjectivity does not coalesce separately from the objective world: one does not know self; one only knows "other." A form of subject–object separation, mythologically understood, is the halving of Urperson into male and female, Eve's being made from Adam's rib. Adam, with his female rib, personified an original androgynous (better: Urperson) unity. But pre-separation, pre-Fall Urperson is static, innocent, naive, unconscious, non-oppositional. With the expulsion from Eden, universal sexual desire, present in all animal and plant life, takes on meaning; it becomes the expression of the psychic hunger for return to what has been lost. The situation is, once again, paradoxical: the Fall is "up" since it brings consciousness; it is "down" as it denotes conflict, striving, the endless faulted human search for a partner who will restore wholeness. Archetypal, undivided Urperson stands behind and beneath sexual desire as its instigating source, the mythological basis for instinctual need as it appears in human beings. We who are mythological descendants of Adam and Eve carry in us the joy and the agony of this primal sexual wounding and resultant restless search. Every darting, hungry eye is its expression.

Inextricably interwoven with sexuality, the separation of Urperson expresses as well the separation of good and evil and, with it, the dawning of moral consciousness. Loving, angelic, song-singing Urperson is good. Fallen angels, dark spirits, all kinds of nefarious power influences coalesce into an image of the devil. Before the Fall in the Garden of Eden, though a nascent separation of genders is present, there is no awareness of the desperation that is invariably mixed into human sexual hunger. Male and female are unselfconscious about nakedness, a factor of their psychological innocence. As the Fall with its disobedience enters the picture, so also does the experience of good and evil, of loneliness, of the use—and misuse—of sexual desire as the instinct for restoration in human relationships. As loneliness prompts us to risk in loving, we retrace the steps of biblical mythology, fingers crossed against the traces of evil that show themselves. This archetypal dynamic—original wholeness, separation, efforts toward restoration, failure, re-trial—forms the background for the image of Second Adam/Urperson/Christ in the Isenheim Crucifixion.

Evil and the feminine are unconsciously associated in the

Western tradition, dominated by the Genesis story and its Father God. Both evil and the feminine are separated from an original androgynous unity, which has served to connect them in the Judeo-Christian unconscious. According to Genesis, Eve was created out of Adam's body and fell for the delicious fruit of knowledge. Acting as the devil's handmaid, Eve seduced Adam, causing the Fall and, presumably, all subsequent sexual grief. This is our inheritance from what I have called, elsewhere, "present consciousness," our cultural, patriarchal conditioning.[8] To this exhausted rationale, Grünewald's Isenheim Crucifixion provides a jolting alternative. Rather than reiterate the orthodox split in gender and morals, and the consequent feminine guilt that might be expected, Grünewald moved in a totally different direction.

Jung draws a remarkable series of conclusions from his analysis of *Interrogationes maiores Mariae*, a gnostic vision quoted by Epiphanes (Epiphanius), an Alexandrian Gnostic of the early Christian era.[9] His work is pertinent to my concern here with Urperson as inclusive of evil and sexuality, rather than androcentric and clean. As Epiphanes' vision was related by Jung, "Christ took this Mary with him on to a mountain, where he produced a woman from his side and began to have intercourse with her." The vision goes on to say that Mary—whoever she was—was in such a state of shock that she fell to the ground. Whereupon Christ said to her, "Wherefore do you doubt me, o you of little faith?" According to Jung, in a seemingly strange leap, this is a reference to John 6:53, "Unless you eat the flesh of the Son of man and drink his blood, you have no life in you."[10]

The emergence of the woman from Christ's side identifies him as the First Adam, the original Urperson, pre-gender.

Out of undifferentiated unity, the feminine emerges as separate; Adam is then masculine and Eve feminine. Creation occurs. Urperson, through dislodgement of the feminine, splits into two sexes. The Second Adam, in this gnostic tale, restores the original unity through the action of sexual mating, making once again whole what had been separated in the first creation. Disobedience–the Fall–is present in his showing the sexual union to Mary, suggesting the evolution of a new level of consciousness. Both creation and intercourse express the power of instinctual nature and point to an archetypal level of psyche being demonstrated. "[W]hat the psyche has made of the instinctual impulse" (Jung's words) is expressed in a way that anyone who has ever been in the throes of sexual fervor can grasp.[11]

Mary cannot believe her eyes–Christ having sex with a woman he produces from his side for Mary to witness. She faints; "the meaning is still hidden from consciousness," according to Jung.[12] Christ recapitulates the mythos. The vulgarity of showing, out-front without the veil of nicety, points to the ordinariness of the mystery; the symbol is as everyday as one's sexuality. Ego consciousness faints with shock. Jung makes my Anglican heart glad as he takes the process a step further. He suggests that the scene anticipates the eucharist, the ingestion of body and blood of the Self, with its startling corporeal implication. A communicant participates in reunion by physically eating and drinking the common bread and wine which are the presence of the reunited Urperson.

Mary is stupefied humanity, caught as it is in a divided world, mistaking appearance for substance. There is no protection of poor Mary's sensibilities in this vision, even as life itself does not protect innocence. Rather, Jesus' slice into the fabric of conventional wisdom is a rough challenge. Mary and the reader are given the opportunity to grasp the secret of Urperson and its quite simple, quite natural, mystery.

Applying this gnostic story to the Isenheim Crucifixion moves me closer to the revelation inherent in Grünewald's Christ. The ego may look at the painting and fall to the ground in shock, as Barbara and I almost did in 1976, so gruesome is the portrayal and its draw from the roots of the unconscious. The ego may, of course, see nothing but a famous painting. But if the soul begins to awaken, it may, indeed, faint, as did gnostic Mary. A torrent of confusion, the firstfruits of recognition, might ensue. Mary saw Christ using his sexuality as restoration, uniting him with the feminine removed with his rib. In my imagination, Grünewald painted a syphilitic Christ, assuming a sexually active Jesus, thus adding an additional dimension to the *conjunctio* present in the gnostic tale.

Salvation then, understood as one's participation in the deepest, most pervasive spiritual reality, is not a rescue from darkness. Not if Christ is the Second Adam.

Salvation, as I use it in a psychological sense, is the personal, often private, even secret, inner knowledge – always based upon experience – that dispels illusion. The knowledge of impending death can be saving if one embraces "the next step" as a natural threshold. So Jesus confesses upon the cross, when help is past: "Father, into thy hands I commend my spirit" (Luke 23:46). In the Isenheim Crucifixion, evil as destructive illness, portending death, is intrinsic to Urperson. Christ, as shown by Grünewald's Crucifixion, suffers as humanity suffers; the hospital patients suffer as Christ suffers. Christ is humanity as God; humanity is God as humanity.

The fate of a divided and reuniting Urperson, Jung's Self as the transpersonal center of the personality, is illness, suffering, death. It is not so much generosity that we see in the Grünewald Crucifixion, a divine figure demonstrating noblesse oblige. Rather it is God participating in the mystery of evil inextricably coexisting with good. The notion of grace is redrawn. Grace becomes salvation through the realization that there is no deliverance from evil, nor need there be. A vein of evil is present in every act of creation and love.

A potent discovery. The blandishments of conventional salvation—a good and perfect God will carry me—seem almost infantile. So also do the blandishments of ego, that one is personally responsible for a fateful encounter with evil, that one stepped onto Pan Am 103 with a karmic intentionality aimed at doom. Paradisiacal expectations are cut to the quick; there are no coattails one can ride, not even one's own. Paradox comes more clearly into view. One participates in good by immersion in evil; one stumbles into evil in the search for good. Evil's presence is as ubiquitous in life as is blessing. In a full deck of cards, the Joker and the Ace are always present.

I have in my study a poster advertising a production of *The Constant Prince*, a medieval play performed in New York in the late '60s by the Polish Laboratory Theatre directed by Jerzy Grotowski. I saw it presented in the Washington Square Methodist Church in Greenwich Village. An arena was built in the center of the church with bleachers on all four sides of a simple performance space with only a table in the center. The language spoken by the half-dozen actors was Polish, but I did not need to understand the words. The play was an allusion to the mythologem of Christ.

As I remember the play, the prince was a good man who was set upon by his people. At the end, the dead prince lay naked upon the table. We were told that he would stay there until the audience was gone. Slowly and silently the audience dispersed. I could not move. I was transfixed. After some time, a member of the staff asked me if I would please go.

The play suggested the old paradigm: mean people against good leader, evil triumphing over good. My poster, however, suggests a deeper meaning, making the mystery more explicit. The dead prince lies within a circle and a square, arms and legs spread, as in the Leonardo portrayal of Urperson. In the opposite direction, overlapping at the groin, with its feet behind the prince's head, is his mirror image, a shadow of himself, as black as the prince's body is white. That is the Grünewald message: good and evil are joined in Urperson, the union of opposites. And the groin is the place of meeting.

Jung wrote:

> Once the exploration of the unconscious has led the conscious mind to an experience of the archetype, the individual is confronted with the abysmal contradictions of human nature, and this confrontation in turn leads to the possibility of a direct experience of light and darkness, of Christ and the devil. For better or worse there is only a bare possibility of this, and not a guarantee; for experiences of this kind cannot of necessity be induced by any human means. . . . It is more what we would call fate. . . .
>
> Without the experience of the opposites [i.e., Christ and the Devil] there is no experience of wholeness and hence no inner approach to the sacred figures. For this reason Chris-

tianity rightly insists on sinfulness and original sin, with the obvious intent of opening up the abyss of universal opposition in every individual. . . . in the [S]elf good and evil are indeed closer than identical twins! The reality of evil and its incompatibility with good cleave the opposites asunder and lead inexorably to the crucifixion and suspension of everything that lives. . . . the truth about the self [Self]–the unfathomable union of good and evil– . . . [is its] antinomial character . . . which is itself both conflict and unity.

Christianity has made the antinomy of good and evil into a world problem and, by formulating the conflict dogmatically, raised it to an absolute principle.[13]

Erotic love forces itself upon human beings as Jung's "inner approach to the sacred figures" of Christ and the Devil, good and evil. On this Freud and Jung agree, but on different levels of interpretation. For Freud, the issue is the extent to which the ego is tortured and sickened by forbidden and repressed instinctual desire. For Jung, the conflict (even when conscious) reflects the nature of psyche itself, and awareness heightens the conflict rather than promising escape. Salvation comes in the *meaning* brought by awareness. Relief comes in accepting the instruction of experience, without reducing it to make it palatable. Grief is not, finally, ad hominem, a personal neurosis, a punishment for individual sin. Grief is a condition of life.

One's *knowing* in grief is gnostic, as Jung implied when he wrote, above, that "experience of this kind cannot of necessity be induced by any human means," nor can it be rationally or empirically demonstrated. The awakening of desire, sexual joining, and living out the complexities always present in desire and union are psychologically based upon an inner presence of Urperson, experienced through the body and the mind's natural participation in good and evil.

6

CHRIST, SEXUALITY, AND DISEASE

The paradoxical nature of God has a like effect on man:
it tears him asunder into opposites and delivers him over
to a seemingly insoluble conflict.

C. G. Jung,
CW II, §738

. . . all manner of good as well as evil . . . break through
in us, particularly in regard to love.

C. G. Jung,
CW II, §742

(AN ONGOING COMPLEXITY IN THIS WORK HAS BEEN THE
name I use for the figure on Grünewald's cross: Jesus, the
English translation of his given name; or Christ, a title meaning the anointed one, the more traditional way of referring
to Jesus as the Son of God. I have chosen to call him Jesus
when my emphasis is more biographical and historical, if, indeed, the scriptural account can be understood as that. Christ
is used when the emphasis is trans-historical, mythic, doctrinal; where the figure is seen more as an image of the Self
than as a man who presumably lived at a certain point in time.
The two names inevitably cross over one another, since it is
impossible to speak of the man without also implicating the
symbol, given the cultural importance of the image.

Moreover, since the Church understands the Nazarene
to be both man and God, indivisibly, when one writes from
within the Christian tradition the two emphases can never

be entirely distinct. The reader will have discovered that I take the Church's doctrine of the Incarnation seriously and that my investigation of the Grünewald Crucifixion depends upon it. Moreover, as a Jungian, I understand that every human being is symbolic, simultaneously pointing to and expressing a psychic mystery. Both my Christian experience and my Jungian orientation stand behind that conviction.)

We now enter the imaginal heart of the matter. I wonder about Jesus' sexuality and its relationship to his Grünewaldian disease. I wonder about various possibilities of Jesus' erotic relationships, whether literal or metaphoric, with the four figures surrounding him on the Isenheim Crucifixion panel. With Christ at the center, the four other persons arranged about him are energy-infused points on a psychological mandala. They are involved in his life and his death—and, perforce, his sexuality—powerfully and primally. They are constituent parts of the archetypal psychology of the panel.

CHRIST AND SEXUALITY

Sexuality is both blessing and curse. It is blessing as creation of new life—when that life is wanted and cherished. It is blessing as excitement—drawing us out of ourselves toward intimacy with another. It is blessing as rhythm—movement from stasis to interest to desire to engagement to play to ecstasy to orgasm to rest. It is blessing as entrée into another world—a world of other-than-ego. Sexuality is blessing because it is the body-point of love. Desire is the signal of archetypal presence.

Sexuality is curse because it promises new life but brings none, or brings more than we can cherish, or brings responsibility beyond our capability. It is curse as pressure – body impels us, forces us, demands obedience, then leaves us to deal with the fallout for the rest of our lives. It is curse as mind separating from body separating from soul – a driven, non-cooperating confusion. It is curse as age diminishes body as desire remains young. It is curse as illness lurks within its sweet promise.

Sexuality is, as Eliade wrote, hierophanic and cosmological – it manifests the sacred, it makes the world.[1] Sexuality's world "wake(s) the lover with amazing joy," in the words of St. John of the Cross;[2] it comes to life as innocent child and as oozing perversity, demonstrating the characteristics of a beneficent and demonic god. Sexuality is an alchemic vessel; the mixtures in the container are both volatile and inert. They explode in tyranny and corruption; they do not move at all. Desire enters us, distorts us, causes us to draw back in fear, insistently urged on by an instinct that is autonomous, coming from a place we do not know. We brush Urperson – the cosmic original image – in our mindless regressions, flashing, disappearing, leaving us hungry when fulfilled, fulfilled while still hungry. Sexuality is simultaneously a function of time and space, of soul and eternity, the incarnation of soul and the ensoulment of body.

John of the Cross, again:

> O living flame of love,
> how tenderly you wound
> my soul in her profoundest core!

You are no longer shy.
Do it now, I ask you:
break the membrane of our sweet union.

. . . Killing, you turn my death to life.

. . . O soothing cautery![3]

It is incomprehensible that instinct be incongruent with nature, whether or not nature is understood as sacred. Put another way, the sexual act, the means for extending life into another generation, the primal human avenue to transpersonal experience, as John of the Cross knew, cannot be ungodly. Rather it may be quite the opposite, a taste, a foretelling, of death, the renunciation of ego, the doorway to soul. André Gregory, the playwright/director, put it this way in *My Dinner with André*:

You know, in the sexual act there's that moment of complete forgetting which is so incredible, and in the next moment you start to think about things . . . the world comes in quite fast. Now, that may be because we don't have the courage to stay in that place of forgetting, because that is again close to death.[4]

Humanity's propensity to surround sexuality with prohibitions, secrecy, and awe attests to its importance as fundamental to life itself. And since sexuality is fundamental, it is enmeshed in moral paradox, good and evil, blessing and curse. Christ as Urperson, human figure seen as archetypal power, "the author and finisher," "the Alpha and Omega," cannot be abstracted from the most powerful human drive, source of the most powerful human emotions. The denial is as damaging to the human spirit as the removal of evil from a central place in one's understanding of psychic reality. What is natural and necessary to life, then, must be included in the Christ-image. Otherwise, the split remains; we are disengaged from the cosmology of our own being. And, if Eliade is to be believed, we miss the world-building manifestation of the sacred in human life.

I must suppose that the Jesus of Grünewald's imagination felt and functioned sexually as a male prior to the illness depicted in the Crucifixion painting. Only then can that figure be the Urperson as I have drawn it, the mythical model of human life. Whether one can find suggestions of Jesus' sexuality in scripture is almost–but not quite–beside the point, since my work is an exercise in fantasy and imagination, not exegesis. It is possible but not essential to find overtones of intimacy in traditional literature; imagination always intrudes upon orthodox reserve. Fantasy, as I have drawn from it in this work, cannot be linearly or temporally or neatly fit into mainline Christian tradition. Illness, fever, scabs–the disarray of life–infect my imagination as they do Grünewald's Christus and, in Jung's view, the substance of psyche itself.

CHRIST, SEXUALITY, AND DISEASE

Erich Fromm said, "human beings are half animal and half symbolic."[5] It is unexceptional to connect symbol with mystery with Self as god-image. That is the "higher" aspect of humanity, which everyone officially approves. But the

animal part of human nature is another matter. Anyone familiar with the United States Senate hearings for the nomination
of Justice Clarence Thomas got a fast education in a fundamental presupposition of psychoanalysis—what appears and
is acceptable on the surface of life disguises a vast subconti-
nent ordinarily hidden from view. One is repelled by the intrusion of instinct and ego's intrusion upon the intrusion.
Does this belong in decent life? Might Fromm's animality—
animal spirit, a Jungian would say—actually be essential? Yes,
it belongs. Grünewald's painting tells us it belongs—and
belongs in the heart of symbol and mystery.

One comes upon divine love, goodness itself, hidden
within the sores of the Grünewald Crucifixion. Love as hidden as sperm in semen. In obedience to his nature as both
male and Urperson, Jesus lived—and as symbol Christ, continues to live in every person—sexually. (The tense changes
as one moves from historical person to symbol. Gender in-
clusiveness is beyond my capability.) Christ as god-symbol
is love with open arms and heart. Jesus is aware of the desire
that connects him to his symbolic source; he follows desire
in obedience to his nature. The seed of life erupts and leaps
from his body to another, or from another's to his, spring-
ing from depth. In his obedience, Jesus lives the rapture of
God. How else do we know the meaning of rapture?

This Christ is a metaphor of union. Even as Jesus moves
beyond himself in his affection, as the spark of life germinates
and flows from his body to another, so also does the Self seize
the moment of Jesus' desire to enflesh divine love. Presence.
Entry. Union! Yet alas, in the delight of accomplishment,
the specter lurks, ready to strike, making fulfillment the com-
municator of disintegration. The paradoxical aspect of all

things psychological is catastrophically evident and irrationally operative in the height of physical joy. In his obedience to both his human and divine nature, Jesus encounters the terrible, the illness that will make him the ravaged figure we see upon Grünewald's cross. Tragedy becomes apparent. Jesus' witness to his nature is an entry point for evil. The answer cannot be an avoidance of life in order to save life. The virus is everywhere.

Disease becomes, literally for some, metaphorically for everyone, sexual wound. There is no escape from its potential once one moves beyond innocence, beyond the simple purity of the Garden. Jesus as Christ, imaging in himself full humanity and full divinity, brings with him enmeshment in the desire and in the pain that inevitably interlaces desire. The demand of instinct requires risk. Risk introduces danger. Whether completion comes, whether infection, whether dismal failure, wound and sexuality are as much subject and predicate as are delight and sexuality. A woman is fulfilled, yet invaded and burdened. A man expands, explodes, and dies. Each carries the inevitable injury of sexual love. Promise leading to apex leading to flat anti-climax and emptiness leading to new promise is the common round. There is no abundant life without sexuality—no life at all, in point of fact. There is no sexuality without disease. The scabs of the Isenheim Christ, the distorted hands and feet, the green skin— these are evidence of archetypal pattern.

A gay man speaks of the cloud of anxiety he and his partner have in their now-monogamous sexual life. Sex has become a symbol of death. He compares this with their years of sexual freedom—one might call it abandon—shared with many partners in the seventies and early eighties before the

135

plague struck. Sex was fun. Now, even when safe, it is tinged with terror.

Since the advent of AIDS, one can see more clearly that sex was never just fun. The mysterious presences of life and death are inextricably intertwined in celebration and pleasure, in instinct. The virus has always lain in wait, as the Isenheim patients discovered. Precisely because sexuality is sacred power—where animal and symbol coalesce—it always has been a source of human distress as well as gratification. This is the core of Eliade's cosmology, the making of a universe of meaning, a brush with the divine. This is hardly the fault of the homosexual.

For a short time many years ago, I had in my practice a single woman who had had a brief but very powerful affair with a foreign student who was married with several children. She was much in love with this man—and he, apparently, with her—and she remained so, some time after he had left to return to his homeland. Her work with me had to do with her feelings about him, about his leaving her to return home—she presumed to a normal kind of life such as never could be hers again after their relationship. Not only was her affair the "brush" of her life, but also he had left her with child. She was devoted to her son and cherished him as the gift of her life. Yet her struggle to maintain herself and her young one was enormous, the more so as her single parent-hood was completely out of keeping with the ethos of her land. She bore amazingly little ill will, even when her attitude was closely examined in the light of her dreams. What she needed from her analysis was an understanding of her fate, her cosmology, the world that had come about through her obedience to the love that poured forth through her instinct.

As I reflect on that story, I see veins of evil interstitially weaving in and through the connection of that man and woman and the legacy of their brief liaison. Granted, the child was cherished and there was no illness. Yet I was pained at the deadly loneliness that lay in the wake of her love. She was sentenced to a life of hard, even subservient, labor, social rejection, faded memories, missed opportunity—a life-fate as invidious as disease. And the father's obedience to himself produced not only one family for which he was responsible, but a second which he felt he must abandon. What regret, what self-incrimination, was his?

This is more than sex leaving its mark. It is Jung's meeting with the gods in an ordinary life situation, with the gods putting their stamp on at least three human beings. The divine background of love requires passion, the suffering illustrated in the Isenheim Crucifixion. Human yearning, a mild word for the crescendo of expectation that lovers feel, implodes upon everyone invaded by nature's sacred power. We call it infatuation when it is fleeting, falling in love when it has a deeper resonance. The gods reach up and out of their hidden places, with their own yearning, their own desire, even as we reach out to another. I do not see how Jesus could have been god-in-flesh without such need, with its portent of dismay.

An important commentary by Robert Sardello on the cultural psychology of AIDS, "The Illusion of Infection," appeared in *Spring 1988*.[6] Sardello suggests that the modern medical understanding of disease as "an objective entity that has invaded the body . . . [is] a major form of culturally sanctioned soul-suppression." Following Samuel Hahnemann, the founder of homeopathy, Sardello sees AIDS as a contemporary manifestation of "a constantly shifting process,"[7] which allopathic medicine reifies as bacteria and viruses. Modern "cures" are the suppression of the process, effectively driving the illness more deeply into body-soul, emerging in what we currently call cancer, leprosy, and AIDS. He sees these as various aspects of the same process; i.e., "cancer is AIDS and AIDS is leprosy."[8] Paraphrasing Hahnemann, writing of early appearances of disease in the West, Sardello claims that "Itch was the primary malady, with leprosy its physical manifestation."[9] *Roget's Thesaurus* places itch, herpes, erysipilas, and St. Anthony's fire together.[10]

In an intuitive leap, Sardello translates itch as desire, and desire as the driving force behind the building of the Western world. Thus: "The movement of the itch (desire) inward constitutes the history of Western Civilization. Internalizing this disease eventually penetrates the mental plane and from there is exteriorized as the products of civilization."[11] Illness, as enemy, serves to keep desire hidden, which is then polluted and distorted by commercialization. The metaphor is cyclical, integrative of body and soul, imaginatively psychoanalytic to its core. Sardello states,

> Any attempt to cure a disease by an outside agent is bound to produce other diseases that are alterations of the first.
>
> Disease is our fundamental condition, our built-in psychotherapist, our constant spiritual advisor. . . . We are . . . neglecting to honor disease.[12]

Sardello's view is entirely congruent with mine in this work, with one possible exception. While he holds that disease is a natural process, he seems to suggest that health—as the absence of illness – is attainable, if humanity were to listen to disease and learn from it. He goes more than half-way: "Disease is our fundamental condition." Then he draws back: ". . . our built-in psychotherapist." If Sardello envisions psychotherapy as cure, in the sense that cure eliminates disease, he appears to be caught in the conventional paradigm himself. The Isenheim Crucifixion suggests, on the other hand, that healing is not cure, that there is no way to live desire and not also and thereby encounter illness. Illness is not only "our fundamental condition"; it is psyche's, the Self's, fundamental condition.

Malignancy is carried by every person, awaiting birth as physical, emotional, mental turmoil. We carry malignancy as incarnations of psyche. Though the Church teaches that baptism cancels the stain of original sin, no baptism cancels evil, as the crucifixion amply demonstrates. The awful truth is that evil lies hidden in the moist connections of love, hosted by our bodily fluids. Ignorantly, self-righteously, we point accusatory fingers at the deviate, as though the cause lay in loving a forbidden person. It was no insult to God for Grünewald to paint a syphilitic Christ image for the outcast. The outcast incarnates God. Grünewald's Christ touched and touches those who know illness from the inside out, a knowledge so startling that only one caught by his own plague can fathom the depths of its finality.

Some of the danger of sexual risk might be known beforehand, but all of the risk can never be known. A requirement to sacrifice – our need for safety, for example, or the temptation to hide – is stubbornly present in the urgings of eros. Perhaps one is drawn to a disapproved person. Perhaps one will fall in love: one's soul, then, is entangled with another's. A child may come, needing care and labor for decades. Infection couches, costing health, costing life, or the health and life of a loved one. Ego's pretension to autonomy is always surrendered: here is love as great teacher. Yet there is no alternative if one is to be faithful to the insistence, the stirrings, of nature. If one hangs back, one risks losing even more–an elemental meeting with god-in-instinct. Sacrifice sits poorly on modern ears, but it is forever implicit in any sexual encounter. Love, even in the guise of tawdry sex, takes us beyond ourselves, our ego protections, into a land beyond our control.

In consensual sexual love, partners offer their personal integrity, dismantle, expose themselves to intrusion, gamble their substance–all elements of sacrifice. Searching, groping, exploring are confessions of incompleteness. The rhythms of abandon, the desperate thrusting, rolling, opening, presenting–the flows of moisture–are submissions, dances, admissions of need. At each ejaculation into another, a male gives up sperm, his essence, surrendering them to fate in the body of another. At each reception, a female enters into the archetypal pattern of nurture; her life is never only her own again. At each orgasm, ego is washed aside, subjected to verity: "Types and shadows have their ending/For the newer rite is here."[13]

In some part of oneself, one is always at the mercy of another, both human and divine, in making love. Through this crack one tastes eternity. The sacred enters the well-protected precincts of consciousness, and if love is to work, consciousness surrenders.

THE ARCHETYPAL—AND HUMAN—FIGURES SURROUNDING THE CHRIST

Jesus' living his sexuality can be understood both literally and metaphorically. Here my fantasy moves into high gear.

A literal leap: Jesus' sexual relationship with John the Evangelist is homosexual, that with Mary Magdalena is heterosexual. His sexual relationships with Maria, the mother, and John the Baptist are metaphoric, heterosexually and homosexually so, respectively. Imagination is stretched to the breaking point by positing a literal sexual connection between Jesus and his mother; not so improbable, perhaps, is the intimation of a liaison between Jesus and the Baptist. In the psychoanalytic world of the twentieth century, it comes as no surprise that a psychological connection between Jesus and his mother and Jesus and his father/mentor might have an erotic implication.

John the Evangelist

On either side of the crucified Christ on the Crucifixion panel are masculine figures, John the Baptist on Christ's left and John the Evangelist on his right.

The Evangelist has his attention directed to Maria the mother, whom he cradles in his arms. His face is wreathed in agonizing sorrow with a look of petulance. His eyelids are heavy in a feminine way, laden with feeling. From his eye a silk-thread tear drops. His hair is lank and flimsy. He is wrapped in a closely held brilliant red cloak. The folds of the garment move across his right shoulder toward his heart, repeating the feeling motif. He holds Maria in her faint. But how he holds her! They appear engaged in a dance of death, the Evangelist supporting and directing their movement. Maria is in his care, as Jesus directed in John 19:26–27: "Woman, behold thy son! . . . Behold thy mother! And from that hour that disciple took her unto his own home." His mouth open in a moan, he is the only male on the Crucifixion panel showing emotion.

The Evangelist's arms are remarkable. They are vastly elongated; if allowed to hang, they would fall well below his knee. His right arm curves around Maria bracing her against a fall. His left hand grabs Maria's left hand below her wrist, as though to control and restrain her reaching out. Yet, strangely, he seems not to be in a position of authority relative to Maria, but rather her loyal and devoted servant. He is taking the place of her son.

Who was the Evangelist to Jesus? In John's own version of the gospel, he calls himself—extraordinarily, singling himself out as special to Jesus—"the disciple whom Jesus loved . . . which also leaned on his breast at supper."[14] Dürer produced a telling woodcut of the Last Supper in which the Evangelist is asleep on the Master's chest as though he were a child. Jesus both protected him and pushed him into responsibility.

Grünewald's portrayal of the Evangelist as a weeping lad, together with his biblical designation as the "beloved disciple," suggests that the Evangelist played the part of *paidica* (*eromenos*) to Jesus' *erastes*. Thorkil Vanggaard, the Danish psychoanalyst, reports these terms as used by the Doric Greeks as early as the sixth century B.C.E. to refer to a paternal relationship between an older and a younger man, whereby the younger man was initiated into *arete*, or noble manhood.[15]

This Doric relationship involved serious mutual responsibilities on the part of both males, echoed in Jesus' instruction to the Evangelist concerning Maria. Sexual activity was common; the elder inseminated the younger, thus imparting the elder's manhood to him. The Evangelist was philosophically Greek and wrote in that language. Grünewald painted the heads of Christ and the Evangelist parallel to one another, further arguing a relationship between them.

The figure of the Evangelist is one form of Jesus' shadow. He represents an aspect of Jesus' masculinity omitted from the limited confines of the Crucifixion image, perhaps an aspect closely reflective of Grünewald's own personality. The artist, reaching toward a complete image of Urperson, pulls the Evangelist into a mirrored position to Christ, painting him as leaning over the Virgin as if they were about to embrace. He weeps as she faints; they are in symbiosis. What we have here is other than the once-strong man on the cross, who gave his mother away. The Evangelist is adolescent, *puer aeternus*, the boy so attached to the mother that he stays her son, psychologically drawing on her power. An older man might well be attracted by the puer's young masculine pattern of seemingly endless exuberance, élan vital, optimism, strong feeling. While the archetype is dormant within himself, he projects it in his affection for, his protection of, and, finally, his dependence upon the young man.

The older man might hunger for the youthfulness he left behind as he matured. He might seek to recapture what has disappeared in himself. This dynamism within the masculine personality is similar to the need a male feels for the lost feminine in gender separation. An older man's impulse to help and guide a boy is a factor of his unconscious identification with him. The motif of positive shadow integration is played out on Grünewald's screen. The Evangelist, in this psychological sense, is not a person separate from Jesus but a suggestion of Jesus' own wholeness, impossible to portray in a single human figure. The archetypal range of masculinity, from boy to young man to adult to age, is partially caught by Grünewald's characterization of the Evangelist on the panel.

But the knife cuts both ways. The Evangelist is also delicate, and his tenderness is a factor of his closeness to Maria. It creeps up into him from the Virgin. His support of Jesus' mother sponsors his puerishness; in a way, he belongs to her even as she now belongs to him. As with many men who have remained too long within the psychological orbit of the mother, the Evangelist's masculinity is frail. That is the condition the Greek *erastes* tradition of the older man was meant to rectify. The situation is complicated by Jesus' request that the youth care for Maria after his death, putting the Evangelist into a double-bind. Jesus gives strength to the youngster and also continues his tie to the mother. I have wondered if this also might be a reason for the anguish on the Evangelist's face.

A man's need to embody his erotic feelings for another male is a factor of his subjective incompleteness as a male. His desire to embrace, to possess, to depend upon the possessed serves his need for personal wholeness. It fills his masculine gap, particularly urgent were the picture of Jesus meant to convey his status as Christ/Urperson. Jung's concept of the shadow as a split-off opposite to the ego, but shallowly buried from view, lends itself to an understanding of homosexuality. There is, of course, a wide range of homosexual feelings in men and as wide a range of behaviors. The common denominator in homosexual desire, as in all sexual desire, is the hunger, expressed instinctually, for completion and restoration. Instinct in the service of individuation – the completion of the personality – is what I have previously called in this work "obedience to nature." Jesus' love for the Evangelist cannot, in this sense, be considered an emotion instigated only by his noble generosity. In spite of his *erastes* role, there is a note of Jesus' personal need, reflected in his assignment of Maria to the Evangelist.

The archetype of the *puer aeternus*, the eternal boy, clearly present in Grünewald's Evangelist, engages Jesus. The gospel accounts of Jesus' life suggest that he was not emotionally immature; certainly Grünewald did not paint him as such in his Crucifixion. The dead Christ is a fully developed adult man. Yet every man who notices a tinge of nostalgia within himself is in touch with his interior puer. Nostalgia can be traced to the archetypal mother; she is the original container of life, the imago of comfort and self-giving generosity. The puer's proximity to the mother becomes a psychological conduit back to her for a man who loves the puer and who has been separated from her by the distance of his maturity. Grünewald expressed this dynamic in his Crucifixion panel. The faces of Jesus, the Evangelist, Maria, and the Magdalene are parallel to one another and tipped toward the viewer's left, the position of the primal maternal in psychological picture interpretation. Pierced with arrows, Sebastian, possibly Grünewald's self-portrait, fixes his soft gaze upon the foursome from a side panel.

Jesus, in loving a puer, connected himself with a part of the masculine spectrum not obviously present in his vocation as teacher, prophet, messiah – as different from the figure on Grünewald's cross as is Grünewald's portrayal of the

CHRIST, SEXUALITY, AND DISEASE

Evangelist. In this personal sense – "this is who I am within the limitations of one male human figure; he is someone other" – Jesus' love for the Evangelist incorporates Jung's notion of shadow as an undeveloped, left-behind, same-gender side of the personality that requires integration. As the painting strikes me, in loving the shadow/Evangelist, Jesus acknowledges his own human desire and complexity. He also encompasses a broader range of masculinity as Urperson than would Grünewald's cross-figure alone. This will not seem terribly strange to persons who have been in Jungian psychoanalysis. They come to know their shadow as a distinct personal aspect of themselves, providing a wider sense of identity than the ego alone provides.

A puer, on his part, needs a strong masculine force to emulate, thus solidifying his subjective masculine psychological structure, his masculine grid, as I have called it in another work.[16] Tradition suggests that Jesus was superb as a male role model. As presented in scripture, he was strong, intelligent, magnanimous, assertive – altogether a handsomely constructed man. He knew how to love without much worry about what people might think or say about him. In loving a man like Jesus, a puer such as the Evangelist might grow into an appreciation of his masculine inheritance. He is given an opportunity to more readily seize his own manhood.

Maria

My fantasy about Maria has to do with the incest taboo, the deepest, most pervasive prohibition in the conditioned human psyche.

Mother is necessarily involved in any consideration of instinct. In order to conceive, she must be engaged sexually. To give birth, she must deliver part of her body. To feed, she must produce milk and present her substance to her child through her breasts. The effect of Christianity's effectual separation of the Virgin from these natural life processes has been to vitiate her reality as a living female person; she becomes asexual, a spiritual goddess removed from the ordinary lot of women. Indeed, Grünewald's Crucifixion portrayal of Maria establishes this picture of her.

Grünewald's Crucifixion Maria is a wraith, a *fata morgana*. Sinew, blood, and sweat are missing. As a goal for real women, the Church's Maria inhibits enfleshment. The actual mother of experience, knee-deep in drudgery, even the scriptural young woman in labor in a shed on a farm, is hidden behind a veil of purity and untouchability. Only one connection with woman's portion remains: her numbing grief. Grünewald captures the abstraction to perfection in his Maria. We see a woman so encased in aristocratic convention, so masked in the paralysis of sorrow, that she almost ceases to be human.

She is at once the most archaic and the most sophisticated of women. Maria has the facial features and bodily carriage of finely honed nobility, superbly refined. She seems to be turning to marble before one's eyes, with an agony so profound that it is almost beyond emotion, as though at the point of death. The mother precisely reflects the death passivity of her son; from her perspective, he and she are entwined, the same. She feels what he feels; they are united.

Grünewald paints her not so much as a human as an archetype, clothing her in the habit of a nun. Her outer cloak covers a blackish-green garment visible on her arms and inside her veil, encasing her body. The outer dress is made of

circular sections sewn together, suggesting layers of the archetypal mother's presence in the unconscious, her primal
essence as a source of life. Maria's white clothing makes her
startlingly prominent in the panel, drawing one's eyes away
from her son. The archetypal mother in her negative aspect
pulls energy away from her offspring. Loathe to surrender
her ownership of what she has produced, tied to her progeny as extensions of her royalty, the negative mother feeds
on her young, and long past their childhood. In psychoanalytic nomenclature, metaphoric incest produces a son who
is unconsciously tied to his mother, with debilitating consequences continuing long into adulthood. The son's life is
never his own; he is always, in a significant part of himself,
a servant to the queen.

Maria's face is fine porcelain, fragile, taut, with great
strength emanating from below the surface. Waxy tears flow
elegantly down her face; her cheeks are swollen; the skin
around her eyes is dark and, again, circled. Her nostrils are
contracted. From them a fluid drains onto lips that are black,
lifeless. Her face has an odd youthfulness, appearing not much
older than the Evangelist who restrains her or even her son.
Her hands are clenched in desolation, her tie to natural life
gone. Beneath her brilliant appearance, she fades into eternity.

Grünewald depicts Maria as dying a mystical love-death
with her son, suggesting the mythology of Mary, Queen of
Martyrs. Bridget of Sweden has already been mentioned as
a possible source of Grünewald's imagery.[17] In her visions,
Bridget saw the Virgin feeling her son's pain as her own when
she heard his pitiful voice on the cross and witnessed the stif-
fening of his limbs as he died. This is the psychology of
mother–son identification, the symbolic and powerful con-

nection between mythical goddess and son-lover. As Queen of Martyrs, Maria herself experiences the pain of her son's diminishment while simultaneously feeling herself elevated in importance by it.

Mother and son are bonded in an oedipal merger, a not-surprising effect of Maria's supposed separation from Joseph as a conjugal partner. While a son-lover's connection with the mother need not be understood concretely, as in physical incest, the psychological ramifications of metaphoric incest are the same. The concept of oedipal identification had its origin in Freud's drive theory of instinct: love and mutual gratification between mother and son are impelled by the essence of the life force expressing itself in erotic attraction and desire. Jung's movement away from Freud's biology into a more abstract symbolism does not vitiate the intensity of the psychological force, the magnetism, existing between mother and son through their mutual need for one another. The son-lover and the mother flash signals of dependence back and forth, as though they were two sides of the same coin. Grünewald painted Maria and Jesus as symbiotic–dance partners separated by death. The Evangelist, after Jesus' gift of the mother to him, becomes his older brother's stand-in, but nothing is resolved by the transfer. To pry open a separation, a psychological differentiation, in such a situation requires a herculean effort appropriate to the torture of the cross. It cannot be done without a horrendous and ongoing sacrifice. Without this, a male's psychological independence is fragile, with template fissures below the surface of his confidence, ready to crack the surface. Beneath the ego, Freud's incestuous binding thread remains.

One can find suggestions of Jesus' separation from his

mother in scripture. Maria is all but invisible in the years of Jesus' ministry, after his baptism. One exception is her presence at the marriage at Cana.[18] Maria reports to Jesus that the host has run out of wine. Jesus' answer is startling: "Woman, what have I to do with thee? Mine hour is not yet come." Nevertheless, as the classic interfering mother, Maria instructs the servants to do as Jesus tells them. Jesus' response seems abrupt, even cross. In another passage, Jesus' mother and brothers seek him out in the midst of his teaching.[19] Their tenacity moves him to declare that those who "do the will of God" are his true family, thereby frankly turning his back upon his family of origin. Jesus establishes himself apart from entanglement with his mother and relatives.

Grünewald's prominent placement and otherworldly treatment of the Crucifixion Maria underline her importance as personal mother who is also archetypal mother. The Church's message, and Grünewald's cooperation with it, is clear. The way to the Savior is through the Mother, viz., the maternal church. There is no Joseph to obstruct the continuing union of mother–son; neither does Grünewald include a heavenly father as an antithesis. Father-absence aggravates a boy's difficulty in severing the oedipal bond. The tie of mother to son, son to mother, their metaphorical incest– "the deepest tie," according to Jung, and also the most dangerous for a male–is the point at issue.[20]

For a male, avoiding metaphoric incest is a great psychological task, if not *the* great psychological task. Failure in masculinity is always an aspect of mother dependence. A male's deepest sense of gender identity requires a primal coagulation of sacrifice, a discovery of and drawing upon an even deeper source of life-strength than the mother. Psychoanalytically understood, the comfort and security represented by "the mother" are the great impediment to masculine self-regard. For a male to reach for self-definition, for a goal beyond that which is given as birthright, for heroic masculinity, imbeddedness in the mother must be overcome. Jesus' twelve-year-old saying from the Temple, "I must be about my father's business," his silent passage through youth and young adulthood, his times by himself in the wilderness all fit the oedipal-break motif, especially difficult when one's mother is a queen. The hero's fearful night sea journey, the ontological loneliness of living beyond the care of a woman, the isolation of sickness, the risk of death – these are foundational elements for maleness. Maria's grief, losing her most precious possession while simultaneously identifying with his illness and death, is a signal that the mother-archetype is fully engaged in the saga.

Even so, this "deepest tie" remains for Jesus, as it does with every man, no matter how efficient his accomplishment. We find him in Grünewald, as in scripture, in the thick of the struggle. Heroic attainment does not eliminate the mother–son connection: there can be no son without mother, no mother without son; the mother–child pattern is as deeply rooted as life itself. Here is the cosmic struggle in an ordinary human picture-story, a mythologem. It is myth because it tells of "the deepest tie" within a narrative that carries within its organic tissue a general picture of reality.

Looking at the crucifixion, one is carried not only backwards in time to a historical event but also forward into future inevitability; every man who ever lives will face the same struggle with the mother. One moves sideways into an aspect of, say, a neighbor's life, from which grow the wellsprings of empathy. One moves up into a trans-historical pattern, down into a phantasmagoria of human suffering. For the gods, there is no incest taboo. Christ as Urperson can do what he will with the mother–she is subspecies. He can keep her to himself, pass her on to his protégé, acknowledge her queenliness over portions of his domain, claim his kingliness over portions of hers. But Jesus the man cannot. He is subject to human restrictions and incest is forbidden. It ruins what we expect manliness to be.

From one perspective, Jesus' sacrifice on the cross is the climax of his separation from seductive mother-love and is the evidence of his independence as a man. From another, the crucifixion is a lethal wounding which no man who comes into his masculine inheritance can avoid. The cross is the decimation of innocence, the inevitable product of a love that gives its name to mankind's oldest, most stringent taboo. If the desire to join with one's source or one's progeny were not so strong, why would the taboo be universal and everywhere honored? If Jesus did not himself transgress the limitations of mother–son love, how could he represent human enmeshment in the endless permutations of "the deepest tie"? The crucifixion demonstrates the terrible burden that human meaning adds to animal instinct. It portrays personal suffering as more than personal–as deeply patterned archetypal compound, ground in the mortar of desire, reflecting the struggle of psyche itself. The cross reveals person as Urperson, Urperson as person: the mystery of mysteries.

The Church claims to be many things in Christian mythology. Among these is carrier of the mother archetype, responsible for the spiritual and moral well-being of her members. The Church gives birth (baptism), nourishes (holy communion), teaches, binds and unbinds, gathers as clan, returns her children to the earth. But evil is as indigenous to the Church as it is to all of reality; the Church is dangerous as a devouring mother even as she sustains the flicker of life. To be a Christian without an awareness of moral paradox is an invitation to disappointment, anger, blame, and estrangement. Naive Christianity perpetuates an infantile attitude.

For rarely does the Church encourage her children to embark upon a journey bearing any similarity to Christ's sacrifice; even more rarely does she sacrifice her own interests that her child may be emboldened to seek his or her fortune. To find an inner connection with the Self almost always requires a departure, a lone and isolated journey. Not for nothing is the Church collectively characterized as an aristocratic maternal guardian of the status quo, preoccupied with proper behavior, blind to the useless suffering she perpetuates, aware only of herself. She is Maria at Grünewald's cross, in a faint of motherly despair. A nicely packaged Christ is held out as a talisman who will do for us what we are not encouraged to do for ourselves. In a world apart from the ravaged Christus, she does not incorporate him within herself as model. Instead, she clasps her hands in an ecstatic swoon.

Metaphorical incest plays out as Mother Church manages her son, speaking for him, claiming to be his mouthpiece, his interpreter, and arbiter. The tyrannical identification brought on by incest–ownership of the other's body, control of the other's mind, intimidation of the other's spirit–is similar in effect to the pretensions of the Church's claiming to be the mother whom her children must obey, the narcissistic source of their reality. (Protestant denominations have re-formed church structure, but the psychological effects of identification remain, encased in sentimentality: fear of independence, feeding on obligation; depression, splitting, spiritual mediocrity, sacralization of the status quo, as in literal incest.) A captive Christ-son is presented to the world by a Mother Church on her terms, buried beneath ecclesiastic din – the political and financial requirements of the institution.

In her recent book on the Isenheim, Andrée Hayum suggests that the theme of baptism dominates the message of the entire altarpiece.[21] Her interpretation is ironic, for she makes no distinction between an ultramontane, triumphalist understanding of baptism, with its regressive parent–child implications, and the sacrament's incarnational core. Baptism is a ceremonial recognition of the presence of Urperson/Christ in the psyche of the neophyte, acknowledging the portent of authority and dignity as that person evolves as an individual. A positive mother–with the positive archetypal mother functioning as imago within her–knows that her child is not hers to own. She is the launch; the child, carrying her potential into the future, moves within its own fate. Once again, the animal world, with its natural instinctual wisdom, mother separating from offspring when the time has come to do so, is illustrative.

Jesus' connection to and need for the positive archetypal mother is seen in the Church's telling his story and extending his ministry through the centuries, not the least being the service of the Antonian monks in Isenheim. Even as Jesus required Maria for his personal birth and early sustenance, children in need of parenting have properly looked to the Church for care, for learning, for cultic inclusion and meaning. She has celebrated Christ's symbolic presence in the eucharist and nourished him in his body-members, however

CHRIST, SEXUALITY, AND DISEASE

inadequately, for two millennia. She has been good mother as well as bad mother, providing a cultural basis for values and a ritual moment of contact with transcendence. She has erred and her public image is faulted in claiming the sacred to be her possession, in fostering dependence based upon an inflated and pretentious misunderstanding of incarnation. When contemporary Christians, even those who understand themselves as carriers of the Christ image, idealize and identify with Mother Church, they remain bound in her puritanical web, unconsciously possessed and consumed. Christians, regardless of their sincerity, express in their dependence the ruinous psychological consequences of ignoring the incest taboo.

Magdalena

Quite another kind of feminine presence is Grünewald's painting of Magdalena on the Crucifixion panel. She kneels at Jesus' feet, imploring, actively beseeching him not to leave her. Her posture and position in the painting shorten her body; she appears miniscule compared to the gigantic figure on the cross above her. She is not the finely turned out, exquisitely controlled woman Grünewald painted as Maria. There is a difference in class. She is a peasant, coarse, with a plain, flat face and stubby, hard-working hands. Her fingers are grossly entwined, unlike Maria's patrician clasp. There is not a trace of pose; they are flung together in desperation.

Grünewald's way with fingers is striking. All of them are important—the pointing finger of the Baptist, the elongated fingers of the Evangelist, Maria's elegantly fastened fingers, and, of course, Jesus', paralytic and contorted. Grünewald's feminine hands are closed and vaginal, his masculine, open, the fingers separated and phallic. Magdalena's palms are gripped, but her beseeching fingers mirror the tortured, flung-out fingers of Jesus.

Magdalena is a peasant; she is no queen. She, too, is at a loss as to how to live without Jesus, but it is not possible for her to recede into Maria's isolated splendor, an eternal figure carved in stone. She is flesh-and-blood, grasping at life which is being taken from her. Jesus brought her instinctuality to fullness. He was the occasion of her knowing herself as an earthy woman. Luke states that Magdalena was known as a sinner, a woman possessed by seven "evil spirits and infirmities,"[22] deeply affected by her relationship with this man. She may have been the one who bathed Jesus' feet with her tears, wiped them with her hair, kissed and anointed them with a rich ointment from a precious box (Mark 14:3; Luke 7:37–50; John 12:3). The jar on the ground next to her suggests that Grünewald intended this connection.

Were the evil spirits and infirmities sexual? It may have been that Luke considered a grounded sexual woman to be perforce "sinful." Such an implication is in keeping with biblical asceticism. Moving another step, Magdalena may have been a woman with a reputation for living her earthiness with a natural abandon. Instinctuality, as all of life, exists within moral paradox; it cannot be surprising that evil is mixed into the strands of Magdalena's self-expression. Luke also wrote that Magdalena was one of several women who followed Jesus and the apostles about the countryside and that the women "ministered to them of their substance."[23] To have had these women in his company may have been cause for the accusation by the scribes and Pharisees that Jesus ate and drank with sinners, which Luke also reported (5:30). It begins to sound as though Luke had what we might call "an attitude" about carnal women. It need not be ours. Certainly Magdalena was more like the women known by the sick men at the Isenheim hospice than was the untouchable Maria painted by Grünewald.

The color tones of Magdalena's clothing–of the sleeves of her inner garment and the long, flowing outer dress and headscarf–reflect the healthy flesh colors of her skin and hair. They especially contrast with the abstracted white of Maria. Magdalena's hair, particularly, is frankly erotic. It flows below her waist in long brown-blond curls, highlighted by the sun. Her sleeves are gathered in a feminine circularity, repeating the motif used in Maria's cloak, and her arms are raised and joined in a way that suggests an open, available sensuality. Her eyes plead with Jesus. Her mouth twists in desolation. Grünewald may have painted Magdalena as something of an anima-woman, one who projects her personal value upon a man, using her body as her substance; one who has not found her own inner soul or her animus strength and thus must squeeze her self-validation from the man on whom she depends. Or, perhaps, as a woman in the throes of emerging from such a condition.

The earthy Magdalena is a polar opposite to Maria within a feminine continuum. She underlines the motif of instinct in the Crucifixion panel, even as Maria stops it dead in its tracks. A sixteenth-century syphilitic man at the Isenheim hospice gazing upon Jesus and Magdalena saw people like himself and might imagine a saga like his own, all within a sacred precinct. The human emotion in the painting, if nothing else, could move the malediction of the illness into

CHRIST, SEXUALITY, AND DISEASE

a tone of spirit open to transformation, like unto the night peace which can slide into place as death approaches. Understanding, in a rational sense, is not really the factor of change. Certainly the issue is not a knowledge of etiology. Then, as now, physical love is the occasion of delight and life even as it is of suffering and death—a paradoxically painful yet beautiful discovery. The only way to avoid illness is to avoid giving oneself in love. For the ordinary man, this is neither desirable nor possible. The attraction of the projected anima burns with a fierce intensity; nature demands obedience to her call. A man has no alternative to the grief that involvement with another produces in him. The process takes place whether men love women or men love men. For all I know, it may be true for those who love cats.

A moving reference to Magdalena in scripture is the story of her recognition of Jesus after his resurrection. The following narrative is that of the Evangelist in the twentieth chapter of his gospel, so important that it is read at the Easter eucharist:

> The first day of the week cometh Mary Magdalene early, when it was yet dark, unto the sepulchre, and seeth the stone taken away from the sepulchre.
> Then she runneth, and cometh to Simon Peter, and to the other disciple, whom Jesus loved, and saith unto them, They have taken away the Lord out of the sepulchre, and we know not where they have laid him.
>
> . . . Mary stood without at the sepulchre, weeping; and as she wept, she stooped down, and looked into the sepulchre,
> And seeth two angels in white sitting, the one at the head,

158

and the other at the feet, where the body of Jesus had lain. And they say unto her, Woman, why weepest thou? She saith unto them, Because they have taken away my Lord and I know not where they have laid him.

And when she had thus said, she turned herself back, and saw Jesus standing, and knew not that it was Jesus.

Jesus saith unto her, Woman, why weepest thou? whom seekest thou? She, supposing him to be the gardener, saith unto him, Sir, if thou have borne him hence, tell me where thou hast laid him, and I will take him away.

Jesus saith unto her, Mary. She turned herself, and saith unto him, Rabboni; which is to say, Master.

Jesus saith unto her, Touch me not; for I am not yet ascended to my Father: but go to my brethren, and say unto them, I ascend unto my Father, and your Father; and to my God, and your God.

That moment of recognition – "Mary . . . Rabboni" – is electric and telling, to my mind the most poignant in all of scripture. The depth of that meeting, its profound yearning, contains the mystery of man with his soul, of ego with anima, of ego with Self. I recall Paul van Buren, one of the trio of "death of God" theologians popular in the 1960s, even in his strongest anti-metaphysical days, wondering over the phenomenon of recognition. Why is it, he asked, that when one, say, leaves an airliner and walks into a terminal, one face, be it that of mate, friend, lover, child stands out among the sea of faces awaiting the arriving passengers? "Mary . . . Rabboni."

Jesus' response, "Touch me not," intrigues. A relationship that included touching was no longer possible. One can only imagine what kind of body Jesus had after the resurrection; one cannot get even close to the question without imagination. Clearly it is not the same as it had been, since he appeared from nowhere and walked about without physical limitation. This we suppose: a body/spirit transition took place, and an even greater transition, the ascension, was in the making. Love without an involvement of body as we know it is a radically changed love, intimated during life in various ways but rarely welcomed. Mourning, an imposed introverted dealing with loss, replaces extraverted touching. Human beings, creatures of instinct and desire, reach out, as did Magdalena, for the old. And the new. Anatole Broyard, in his extraordinary reflection on his approaching death, wrote,

> My initial experience of illness was a series of disconnected shocks, and my first instinct was to try to bring it under control by turning it into a narrative. Always in emergencies we invent narratives. . . . Stories are anti-bodies against illness and pain. . . . In the beginning, I invented mininarratives. Metaphor was one of my symptoms. I saw my illness as a visit to a disturbed country, rather like contemporary China. I imagined it as a love affair with a demented woman who demanded things I had never done before.[24]

When that is no longer possible, the light of the ego burns more dimly.

Magdalena found in Jesus her way into the place where body opens a door to soul, always the promise of erotic love. Jesus' "touch me not" suggests that, in this post-resurrection meeting, he can no longer come to her as the means of her soul-life; he is no longer physical body. The importance of the physical connection between Jesus and Magdalena is not thereby reduced, for their body connection is what brought Magdalena to her personal knowledge, her gnosis. Here one can see the remarkable spiritual power inherent in physical love. While it is quite obvious that new generations are produced, it is not always so obvious that soul is made, re-made, and re-made again through our touching. When touching is impossible, metaphor as symbol evolves to carry the burden. We invent stories. But the stories are always about love.

One can suppose that Jesus had desire for Magdalena, that he needed her as well. His unconscious femininity, his soul, his anima, in Jung's terms, found expression in his touching, his love for her, his entrance into her world. Roman Catholic theologian Rosemary Reuther in her article "The Sexuality of Jesus" quotes the Gnostic Gospel of Philip: "Jesus loved Mary (Magdalena) more than the other disciples and kissed her many times on the mouth."[25] Also from Philip: "For it is by a kiss that the perfect conceive and give birth." And: "There were three who always walked with the lord: Mary his mother and her sister and Magdalene, the one who was called his companion."[26] Imagining Jesus with ordinary sensual desire, living an ordinary sexual life, joins him with the ordinary human beings for whom he is the symbol of wholeness. To find this scandalous perpetuates the schizoid separation between body and soul that is an even more serious plague than the physical illness depicted in the Isenheim Christ.

John the Baptist

John the Baptist stands on the opposite side of the Crucifixion panel from the Evangelist and the two women. He is turned slightly toward Jesus, but he does not look at him. He seems to be addressing Maria and Magdalena. His face is impassive, as though he were not personally involved in the terrible scene to his right. He is the only figure, aside from the dead man on the cross, who shows no emotion. I will allow my imagination to play with the Baptist's remarkable lack of sentiment.

The tallest of the surrounding figures, the Baptist stands alone, except for a lamb at his feet. He is clothed in animal skins beneath a loose red overgarment; his feet are bare and pointed in opposite directions, his left poised as though not holding his weight. The Baptist's right foot is planted firmly beneath the lamb, whose blood pours from its breast into a sacrificial chalice, a juxtaposition of the old covenant and the new.

The Baptist is a rough man, primitive and natural. He teaches the law, and he indicates the new way—the way beyond his tradition—simultaneously. He holds in his left hand a book, probably the scriptures, and Grünewald has painted his message near his mouth: *Illum oportet crescere, me autum minui*, "He must increase, but I must decrease," from John 3:30, as if it were an instruction for both Maria and Magdalena.

His right arm is the most important element of his portrayal. With his elongated forefinger he points to Christ in an odd and typically Grünewaldian way. The finger has an unnatural upward curvature, even as his thumb unnaturally curves downwards. The two outstretched digits form a kind of fork, repeating the opposition in the Baptist's feet. His pointing finger teaches, indicating the centrality of the crucified one and also the inclusion of both himself and the Evangelist within Jesus' masculine ambit.

From scripture we know that the Baptist was a severe moralist, the most explicit organic connection in the New Testament to the Old. It was he who baptised Jesus, a ceremony centering on repentance, the renunciation of evil, and spiritual birth. The question arose then as it does now: why Jesus, of all people, might need baptism. Need he repent, dissociate himself from darkness as a ruling principle, start anew? If so, the split between good and evil remains — with Jesus separating himself from a humanity filled with pride and sinful disobedience.

Jesus himself gives the answer in Matthew 3:15: "Suffer it [his baptism] to be so now: for thus it becometh us to fulfil all righteousness." "Righteousness" can be understood as referring to authentic psychological "as-is-ness," a showing forth of things as they are rather than what they ought to be as an ideal of moral purity. Jesus witnesses by his baptism to the picture one sees in the Grünewald Crucifixion. The Self totally participates in moral paradox through the intersection of human and divine life, with all of its darkness and light. Error, fault, stagnation, expressed as they are in human illness and in the ubiquity of evil, are woven into the fabric of life, incorporating the highest of the high and the lowest of the low. Jesus' baptism then becomes a statement of the integrity of psychic and physical reality. Nothing is left out.

Grünewald painted the Baptist as unsubjective, outer-directed, thoroughly a man of scriptural authority, the word, with all of the enormous implication of logos-masculinity. His verbal announcement is astounding. The Baptist's staunch moral law, his Hebraic preoccupation with sin and guilt and redemption by purification, is superseded in and by the poisoned Christ. He points away from himself to his brother-shadow, the delicate Evangelist opposite on the panel, as a way into the Christ, brimming with sickness and death upon the cross. The Baptist announces the arrival of the newer rite, moving himself and his tradition to the side. As legalistic shadow figure, he announces that salvation is inclusive, that the sick messiah is the figure of that inclusion. A radical switch has taken place. Righteousness is no longer primarily moral, excluding darkness, a decision for good and against evil, cleaving the world asunder. Authority has made a turn toward the heart.

As with Maria, there is no literal sexual connection between Jesus and the Baptist. Their union is the embrace/kiss of a father renouncing the imperiousness of tradition, his crown of seniority, giving in to a son who contains within himself new potency. Freud was correct that frustration finds its biological source in instinctual deprivation, the seed of new life trapped within a body bound by unnatural convention. But Jung was also correct in shifting biology in the direction of spiritual evil, which, as does frustration, metastasizes into every nook and cranny of human life. The shift was critical, rejoining body and psyche. Jung called ultimate human responsibility for evil a burden impossible for mankind's fragile ego to bear, bursting containment into multifarious shards of psychic morbidity.

For the Baptist, spokesman for God's law, to back off, to point to an image incorporating weakness, required enormous sacrifice, and still does, whenever such a transformation is required. For this to happen, Jesus' more gentle phallic strength had to move into the "driver's seat," so to speak, bringing about the kind of conversion expressed by the words Grünewald painted coming from the Baptist. Such a radical shift in psychological awareness is what Jung had in mind when he recommended that shadow aspects of one's personality become a part of ego consciousness. The more feminine, the more loving and organic, more forgiving-because-related-to-wholeness qualities of the suffering Jesus (which the Evangelist carries as another side of Jesus' shadow) act psychologically as the Baptist's shadow. They mitigate his legal, patriarchal intensity. One might almost say that they open his virginity, his untouched solar-phallic intransigence.

Once again, Grünewald's fingers. Those of the two shadow figures on the panel, the Baptist with forefinger and thumb in opposition, the Evangelist with middle and ring finger separated as he supports and controls Maria, suggest common involvement. It is almost as if the two men signaled one another that they were brothers in their appointed tasks. They have the same name. They have the same hair, red and chopped off abruptly at the nape of the neck. They wear clothing close to the same color, the Baptist's primitive, the Evangelist's sixteenth-century European. The trajectory of the Baptist's finger is exactly parallel to the Evangelist's trunk. Literality and metaphor are interwoven. The down-to-earth Baptist points to Christ, but he also points to the puer Evangelist, which may account for the strange upturn of his finger, even as he speaks to the two women.

The Church understands the Baptist to be a herald, the last in a long line of Hebrew prophets, important because he represents the transition from hallowed tradition to the new age. Within the imaginative choreography of the figures Grünewald painted around Jesus, the Baptist is the only person who could not have been chronologically present in that scene, adding to his symbolic importance. (The Baptist had already been beheaded for the affront of his judgment upon the liaison between Herod the Tetrarch and Herod's brother's wife.) The Baptist's rigorous morality puts him in the father position psychologically, and so the absent father in the panel appears in his guise, accented by the source of light in the painting, emanating from beyond the frame of the painting on the Baptist's left. Father-sternness modulating into, say, forgiveness means that it is no longer enough to fix blame, which would certainly be the case if Jesus were himself afflicted with venereal illness. Many contemporary fathers of sons with AIDS have found this to be the case.

As fathers rarely do, the Baptist diminishes himself before his son, relinquishing his preeminence to the one who is sick unto death. According to Freud, self-diminishment amounts to a man's "femininization" vis-à-vis another man, the result of the passive man's insecurity. What we see in the Isenheim, however, is a strong and uncompromisingly ethical prophet submitting himself to a powerless man not out of inadequacy, but in obedience to a startling new wisdom of the heart. Something happens to the Baptist; he no longer stands only as prophet. He lowers himself from that august position in the Grünewald panel because a new factor has entered the scene. The figure on the cross cuts through moral rectitude. Jesus' authenticity rests upon the inclusion of intimacy, desire, and love, of darkness and weakness, of pathos and suffering in the image of the Self. The Baptist loves Jesus, allowing the supersedure.

That love is not license is attested to by the Baptist's stern presence in the picture. The Baptist's new love is subject to a higher—and, paradoxically, a deeper and lower—feeling authority, based upon instinct or, as Jung understood the matter, archetype. To quote Bob Dylan, "To live outside the law, you must be honest." It is necessary for honesty that love not be separated from its source in body. Only then does it engage soul. Sometimes I find myself imagining that I discern the beginnings of a smile—perhaps of relief—upon his face.

Love obedient to the incarnate Self extracts from both lover and beloved a great price, including the sacrifice of high position. Metaphoric father–son incest, with the father always in control of the son, in-forming him, inseminating him, involves no father sacrifice whatsoever, only father gratification. In the Isenheim, we see the Baptist fading back for his son, something which never happens as long as the father sees himself only as leader. Purification, with its implicit hierarchy of law over sin, is no longer the goal; the Baptist defers to a ravaged man, caught upon the very cross of sacrifice. Grünewald, in placing the Baptist alone but in touch with the lamb, and painting him rough and austere in his teaching role, emphasized the crucial importance of compassion, the product of mutual sacrifice, the product of mutual father/son love.

The reader will have noticed that I consider law giving way to love to have a psychosexual resonance. A father's moving away from his head to follow his heart regarding his son paradoxically expresses the father's phallic strength, for heart is usually considered to be in the realm of the feminine. But the father who accepts his son's authentic manhood and authority as parallel, even superior, to his own can do so only when he is secure in his own masculine grid.[27] If the father is unconsciously preoccupied with his own castration anxiety, he will resist passing his phallic legacy on to his son. The Baptist's remarkable "He *must* increase as I *must* decrease," however, clearly indicates that the potency of Jesus was more important than the Baptist's own status as bearer of the past. In Danish scriptures, the word used for "increase" is *vokse*, which in English can be translated "grow up." The son stands in need of his father's affirmation as a passing on of masculine essence. And the father also desires something of the son — freshness of youth, promise of new generation, vicarious pleasure in accomplishment. Without the son's virility, the father line is at an end. "Must," then, in the Baptist's confession, is an instinctual psychological requirement, a father-son fate.

I once had a problem with an ex-analyst in New York. He charged me for a collegial visit after I had finished my training in Zürich. I told the story of my discontent to a colleague. She wisely said something like this: a man must first learn to surrender to a woman. Then a man must learn to surrender to a man. I thereupon sent a check to the analyst. I may have learned an important lesson in my decrease. Men express their metaphorical homoeroticism by the valence of their social contact with one another, by their exchanges of obligation and respect. If the exchange fails, something essential in the development of the father–son mythos is missed; men become stuck in role playing and in adolescent competition. A psychological metaphor of penetration, a giving and taking of masculine substance, is critical in the masculine world, dominated as it is by phallos. Otherwise, a boy remains psychologically unfilled; he does not open himself to his father. And the older man has no son to whom he can surrender.

To the present-day viewer of the Grünewald Isenheim altarpiece, the message of the ruined Christ can be as new as it was to the Baptist, to the sufferers at the Isenheim hospice, to the young artist from the Bronx. An archetypal expression of essence is present as its influence has grown over the centuries. To those hindered by the stone wall of convention, the Isenheim may not be a panacea, but surely it has become to many a welcome remedy to incessant blame. Sexual energy and spiritual energy, good and evil, light and darkness coalesce in Grünewald's images in a way that can begin to make honest sense. Freud was correct that the power of instinct wages endless war against the power of culture. But Jung was even more correct. These tempestuous opposites can be (and are, finally) harmonized in a uniting symbol even as they are differently perceived.

7

RESURRECTION

GRÜNEWALD'S INTERPRETATION OF CHRIST'S RESURRECTION, on an inside panel of the altarpiece, startles one by its explosion of color and its vibrant contrast with his abysmal Crucifixion. Christ is totally different. A psychedelic explosion bursts upon the canvas. Does it reflect the hallucinatory excursions of sufferers at the Isenheim hospice who were infected by ergot poisoning, with its LSD component? Is this what caused the victims of St. Anthony's Fire in Pont-Saint-Esprit to jump from their windows in terror?

Huysmans says of the Resurrection panel,

> [It] sends you into raptures, for it is truly a magnificent work – unique, I would say, among the world's paintings. In it Grünewald shows himself to be the boldest painter who has ever lived, the first artist who has tried to convey, through the wretched colours of this earth, a vision of the Godhead in abeyance on the cross and then renewed, visible to the naked eye, on rising from the tomb. With him we are, mystically speaking, in at the death, contemplating an art with its back to the wall and forced further into the beyond, this time, than any theologian could have instructed the artist to go.[1]

The blotted flesh of the Crucifixion becomes translucent in the Resurrection. Dark sky remains, but everything has changed. Now appears an entirely different Christ image, surrounded by an aureole of fire, its sparks flying off against the blackness. The upheaval, even convulsion, is glorious, as far away from putrefaction as one could imagine. Volcanic. Cataclysmic. Orgasmic.

Beneath the splendid Resurrection Christ are the more somber earth colors of the tomb, the stone terrain, the Roman legionnaires, repeating the tones in the Crucifixion. They are poor compared to the surrealism of the newly risen and ineffable Christ. They fall, blown hither and yon by the eruption. Grünewald quite obviously painted the men as counterpoints to the spectacular resurrected one. They are as ordinary and transitory as he is emergent and enflamed. Were one to peer into the bowels of the earth, one might expect to encounter such fierce, untamed energy.

The bands of color encircling the trunk, arms, and head of the Resurrection Christ are an aura, "an emanation proceeding from a body and surrounding it as an atmosphere."[2] In the painting, the aura modulates, from the outside in, from the deep blue of the night sky, to day-sky blue, to green, to yellow, to orange-red, to gold—the color of Christ's hair, beard, and upper garment—a gigantic midnight sun. The hues are reflected in the flow of Christ's wrap, the rock behind the gravecloth, the tomb itself, and the armor of the soldiers laid low by its force. This mandalic circle, hazing over the physical outlines of Christ's body, is what caused Huysmans to wax eloquent about Grünewald's status as a painter.

The Grünewald Resurrection colors are the epitome of sunrise seen from the vantage point of the gods. I once arose very early one winter morning on the Rigi, in Switzerland, to see something I'd heard was remarkable. As I stood, a bundle of chattering teeth and bones high above a valley, a ball of fire arose over the opposite peaks, as if shoved up by an invisible hand, bathing the earth in an instant storm of light. I was "blown away," not unlike the tumbling soldiers Grünewald painted in the Resurrection, so sudden was the transformation. As I recall, I literally had to sit down. The juxtaposition of sheer galvanic energy superimposed upon a sleeping and frozen earth was astounding. Many years later I again rose early to stand at the summit of Haleakalo Volcano on Maui, Hawaii. The effect was not nearly the same. The sun rose from the horizon over the sea and moved into the air, dispersing darkness. It was magnificent, the colors were lovely pastel, but in no sense did I feel that I could reach out and touch the vortex of the earth.

What is one to make of the dazzling difference?

In painting his Resurrection as he did, Grünewald con-structed a template beneath which the Crucifixion must be seen as a subtext, a kind of palimpsest. One starts with the Crucifixion and drinks deeply of sickness and death. Then one comes upon a Resurrection, but one that has meaning only when one begins with the prior disintegration. It is crucial to move back and forth between crucifixion and resur-rection, resurrection and crucifixion, in a gestalt where figure and ground play against one another as two sides of the same coin, seen from radically different perspectives. Without a both/and cohesion, a sense of dimension that comes of almost simultaneous interweaving, the Crucifixion repulses one, the Resurrection is a giddy height.

Paradox reaches its apex as the templates superimpose. The bad news of the Crucifixion is good news. The good news of the Resurrection is bad news.

Ergo, illness and death can be good news. There need be no more huge and fruitless effort at seeking a perfect, stainless way, a way that everyone likes and people approve of. There need be no more scrupulosity over mistakes made, since Christ himself, strapped by the human experience, stepped into putrefaction and banality. The void, that which worries us in the dead of night with no sleep possible, is discovered to be as much a part of divinity as it is of humanity. The god-figure itself suffers an end. Blame has its limit when morality incorporates contradiction.

Even as I write this last sentence of my last chapter, I recover, or don't recover, from a heart attack that took place six days after my recent Hawaii sunrise. I wake in the night, sometimes three times, sometimes six, sometimes getting back to sleep, sometimes lying there, reading, gnashing my teeth, staring at the black hole, for hours. Deep night awakeness is terrible. Even semi-sleep is terrible. There are times when I would almost welcome pain.

In the winter of 1992, I attended a memorial meeting in honor of Werner Engel, a pioneering Jungian analyst/physician who died at the age of ninety, having lived a full life which he thoroughly enjoyed, from Berlin to New York, where for years he labored as a hired hand. He was quite a ladies' man; he loved his medical practice, probably before any romantic love. Werner and I had become friends only five years earlier, long past the time when he was a personage. I found the Baptist in him; what I have written here about the sacrificing father archetype is, in a sense, my tribute to him. The New Year's Eve a year before he died, he had telephoned me at 10:30 P.M. in Pennsylvania, when Barbara and I were in the midst of a dinner with a Methodist minister and his wife, long-suffering apostles of liberation. He said only: "Eugene, this is Werner. I want to say one thing to you. Whatever you want to do, do it soon. Don't postpone it. Happy New Year. This is Werner. Goodbye."

At the memorial meeting, his son told his father's last words, said after passing back and forth at the end of a grueling illness: "It's better here."

The glorious sunburst is also bad news. The path to ecstasy is a bumpy road of suffering. However glorious the moment of orgasm, when the door opens to the other world, the moment is gone in an instant. Beneath the toils of illness, inseparable from love, a glimpse of completion opens. Reaching the summit, entering the glorious sunburst, portends a descent to the valley. There is a knowledge, and a secret inner pleasure in the knowing, that pain and pleasure cannot but overflow one another. Night comes. When one is as old and as wise as Werner, one can pass on the knowledge that the dead of night "is better." A son had better take that and give praise in return.

There is more. Grünewald's Resurrection figure is an effeminate Christ, far from the firmly muscled male of the Crucifixion. The Resurrection body dances in the air lightly and gracefully, gaily. There is a sweetness about the Christ's face reminiscent of sentimental Thorwaldsen statues endlessly reproduced in Midwestern Lutheran churches. Christ's gravecloth swirls up out of the newly opened tomb and flies back into the wind. The arms are not those of the Crucifixion, nor are the hands or legs or feet. They are lithe and pale and delicately constructed. His face is vague, almost empty.

Grünewald painted in his Resurrection figure an amalgam of masculinity and femininity, swinging distinctly in the latter direction. The reunion of the sexes finds itself demonstrated in Grünewald's Self, anticipated in the actively bisexual—yet clearly masculine—Christ of the Crucifixion. In the Resurrection, clear masculinity tones out. He is no longer clearly he; he is he/she—androgynous. The integration, longed for by soul and body, has taken place, beyond the stasis of gender. The vociferous ranges of emotion appearing in the Crucifixion figures plane into a centered, peaceable, feminine-like countenance. A bit on the weaker side, perhaps, but what calm a bit of weakness brings to a world torn asunder by the endless round of masculine proving!

An analysand to whom I showed the Isenheim in a book told me a remarkable vision he saw in the Resurrection painting. The supine soldier on the left, head turned away, can be found with the protrusion of the hilt of his sword emerging from the neighborhood of his groin, almost where his erect phallos might be. His companion, debilitated by the energy of the outburst above, hovers over the hilt, his head coming down upon it. If one follows the trajectory of the hilt, moving through the head of the companion, one comes upon the flowing gravecloth and beyond that to the glorified Christ and the flashing auroral blast above and around him. "Do you know what this is?" he asked. I sat dumb. "It is the cosmic phallos. It is the archetypal ejaculation."

Still more. Marie-Louise von Franz uses the Grünewald Resurrection to suggest that

the Cosmic Man is not only the beginning but also the final goal of all of life—of the whole of creation. "All cereal nature means wheat, all treasure nature means gold, all generation means man [sic]," says the medieval sage Meister Eckhart. And if one looks at this from a psychological standpoint, it is certainly so. The whole inner psychic reality of each individual is ultimately oriented toward this archetypal symbol of the Self.[3]

I have previously substituted the term Urperson for the long-used Anthropos, von Franz's Cosmic Man, or simply "man," as per Eckhart. The Self as Urperson is the amalgam Grünewald painted in his Resurrection – a sixteenth-century version of the unified archaic image. The Resurrection template, vis-à-vis the Crucifixion, enables one to grasp the whole of Grünewald's architectonic vision as one sees crucifixion "through" the resurrection, resurrection "through" crucifixion. Such a perception is not linear or time-oriented, as if circumscribed by masculine logos. Grünewald's work is cosmic and circumstantial simultaneously, both historic and contemporary. It is synchronistically spiritual and carnal.

My Grünewaldian imagination has not led me to write a work on self-improvement or a religious tract on conventional Christian hope. The Isenheim, Jung, and, more lately, James Hillman have pushed me to realize that genuine knowing begins when sentimentality no longer bars the way. Only a hope against hope, as it were, no longer striving to trust that good must always triumph, is psychologically and spiritually real.

Huysmans's paean of praise to Grünewald and the Isenheim is a fitting conclusion to this work:

Never before had naturalism transfigured itself by such a conception and execution. . . . [Grünewald] was the most uncompromising of realists, but his morgue Redeemer, his sewer

Deity, let the observer know that realism could be truly transcendent. A divine light played about that ulcerated head, a superhuman expression illuminated the fermenting skin of the epileptic features. . . . These faces, by nature vulgar, were resplendent, transfigured with the expression of the sublime grief. . . . Grünewald was the most uncompromising of idealists. . . . He had gone the two extremes. From the rankest weeds of the pit he had extracted the finest essence of charity. . . . In his art was revealed the masterpiece of an art obeying the unopposable urge to render the tangible and the invisible. . . .[4]

NOTES

Introduction

1. I have checked my memory with a number of fellow students at Virginia in those years. Brewster Beach, for one, a Jungian analyst, in a personal communication recalled Mollegen's remarks as I remember them.
2. Anthony Storr, *Solitude* (New York: Free Press, 1988), p. 169.
3. Michael Polanyi, *Personal Knowledge: Towards a Post-Critical Philosophy* (Chicago: University of Chicago Press, 1958), p. vii.
4. C. G. Jung, *Collected Works*, trans. R. F. C. Hull, ed. H. Read, M. Fordham, G. Adler, Wm. McGuire, Bollingen Series XX, vols. 1–20 (Princeton: Princeton University Press and London: Routledge and Kegan Paul, 1953 ff.), vol. 6, para. 622. All further references to Jung's work will be by volume and paragraph numbers.
5. Stephan Hoeller, *Jung and the Lost Gospels* (Wheaton, IL: Quest Books, 1989), p. 7.
6. Polanyi, *Personal Knowledge*, p. viii.

I

1. C. G. Jung, CW 5, §35.
2. Andrée Hayum, *God's Medicine and the Painter's Vision* (Princeton: Princeton University Press, 1989), p. 89.
3. Personal conversation.

4. C. G. Jung, CW 14, §792.
5. C. G. Jung, CW 16, §9.
6. Robertson Davies, *The Manticore* (New York: Penguin Books, 1976), p. 178.
7. John Dourley, *The Illness That We Are: A Jungian Critique of Christianity* (Toronto: Inner City Books, 1984).
8. Eugene Monick, *Castration and Male Rage: The Phallic Wound* (Toronto: Inner City Books, 1991).
9. See Eugene Monick, *Phallos: Sacred Image of the Masculine* (Toronto: Inner City Books, 1987).
10. C. G. Jung, CW 12, §11.
11. Ibid.
12. Davies, *The Manticore*, p. 168.
13. C. G. Jung, *Memories, Dreams, Reflections*, recorded and ed. Aniela Jaffé and trans. Richard and Clara Winston (New York: Random House, 1965), pp. 36–41.
14. See Louis S. Berger, *Substance Abuse as Symptom* (Hillsdale, NJ: Analytic Press, 1991), p. 121.
15. Stephan Hoeller, *The Gnostic Jung and the Seven Sermons to the Dead* (Wheaton, IL: Quest Books, 1982), pp. 55–56.

2

1. See Adalbert Mischlewski, "Die Auftraggeber des Isenheimer Altares," in *Grünewald et Son Oeuvre* (Proceedings of the Round Table organized by the Centre National de la Recherche Scientifique at Strasbourg and Colmar, France, October 1974), p. 16.
2. See Albert Chatelet, "Unité ou Diversité du Thème du Retable D'Issenheim," in *Grünewald et Son Oeuvre*, p. 61.

3. See Roland Recht, "Les Sculptures du Retable D'Issenheim," in *Grünewald et Son Oeuvre*, pp. 27 ff.
4. J.-K. Huysmans (essays) and Eberhard Ruhmer (catalogue), *Grünewald: The Paintings, Complete Edition* (London: The Phaidon Press, 1958), p. 27.
5. Ibid., p. 118.
6. Nikolaus Pevsner and Michael Meier, *Grünewald* (London, 1958; New York: Harry N. Abrams, Inc., 1958), p. 21.
7. See Huysmans and Ruhmer, *Grünewald: The Paintings*, p. 27.
8. See Arthur Burkhard, *Matthias Grünewald: Personality and Accomplishment* (Cambridge, MA, 1936; rept. New York: Hacker Art Books, 1976), p. 5.
9. Huysmans and Ruhmer, *Grünewald: The Paintings*, p. 29.
10. Ibid.
11. Pevsner and Meier, *Grünewald*, p. 25.
12. Burkhard, *Matthias Grünewald*, p. 11.
13. Erich Neumann, *Art and the Creative Unconscious*, trans. Ralph Manheim (Princeton: Princeton University Press, 1959), pp. 17–18.
14. Erwin Panofsky, *The Life and Art of Albrecht Dürer* (Princeton: Princeton University Press, 1955), p. 230.
15. It is difficult to know what Burkhard meant by this reference to Grünewald's "dynamic personality." I could say that Grünewald's unpretentiousness drew out a strong archetypal presence from the unconscious and propelled it into his work. Such a process is dynamic in the best psychological sense of that word, but I doubt that my observation is what Burkhard had in mind.
16. Burkhard, *Matthias Grünewald*, p. 4.
17. Eberhard Ruhmer, "Grünewalds Ausstrahlung im 16. und 17. Jahrhundert," in *Grünewald et Son Oeuvre*, p. 173.

18. Kenneth Clark, *Civilisation: A Personal View* (New York: Harper & Row, 1969), p. 148.
19. See Burkhard, *Matthias Grünewald*, p. 6.
20. Eberhard Ruhmer, *Grünewald: The Drawings, Complete Edition*, trans. Anna Rose Cooper (London: The Phaidon Press, 1970), p. 20.
21. C. G. Jung, CW 6, §622.
22. Ibid.
23. Ruhmer, "Grünewalds Ausstrahlung," pp. 173–74.
24. Panofsky, *The Life and Art*, pp. 24–25.
25. Huysmans and Ruhmer, *Grünewald: The Paintings*, pp. 24–25.
26. See ibid., p. 120.
27. J. H. Plumb et al., eds., *The Horizon Book of the Renaissance* (New York: American Heritage Publishing Co., 1961), p. 103.
28. H. W. and D. J. Janson, *Picture History of Painting, from Cave Painting to Modern Times* (New York: H. N. Abrams, 1957), p. 116.
29. Ibid., p. 137.
30. Clark, *Civilisation*, p. 155.
31. Wylie Sypher, *Four Stages of Renaissance Style: Transformations in Art and Literature* (Garden City, NY: Doubleday, 1956), p. 36.
32. Ruhmer, *Grünewald: The Drawings*, p. 9.
33. *The New Cambridge Modern History*, vol. 1, *The Renaissance* (Cambridge: Cambridge University Press, 1957), p. 78.
34. Ibid., p. 82.
35. Ibid., p. 86.
36. *Encyclopedia Britannica*, vol. 10 (Chicago: Encyclopedia Britannica, 1960), p. 240.
37. *The New Cambridge Modern History*, vol. 1, p. 215.
38. Ibid., p. 92.

39. Thomas F. Graham, *Medieval Minds: Mental Health in the Middle Ages* (London: Allen & Unwin, 1967), p. 79.
40. Clark, *Civilisation*, p. 141.
41. Burkhard, *Matthias Grünewald*, p. 84.
42. Huysmans and Ruhmer, *Grünewald: The Paintings*, p. 14.
43. Pevsner and Meier, *Grünewald*, p. 19.
44. Emma Jung and Marie-Louise von Franz, *The Grail Legend* (New York: Putnam, 1970), p. 214.
45. See chapter 5 of this volume, the section on "Urperson and Salvation," for the story of the coining of this word.
46. Neumann, *Art and the Creative Unconscious*, pp. 94–95.

3

1. *Webster's Collegiate Dictionary*, 5th ed., p. 336.
2. C. G. Jung, *Memories, Dreams, Reflections*, p. 185.
3. C. G. Jung, CW 9, i, §5.
4. Quotation unrecovered.
5. John Money and Anke A. Ehrhardt, *Man and Woman, Boy and Girl* (Baltimore: Johns Hopkins University Press, 1972), p. 36.
6. See Andrew Samuels et al., *A Critical Dictionary of Jungian Analysis* (New York: Routledge & Kegan Paul, 1987), pp. 73–74.
7. C. G. Jung, CW 13, §457n.
8. C. A. Meier, *Ancient Incubation and Modern Psychotherapy* (Evanston: Northwestern University Press, 1967), pp. 123–24.
9. C. G. Jung, CW 9, ii, §356.

10. Edward S. Casey quoted in James Hillman, *Re-Visioning Psychology* (New York: Harper & Row, 1975), p. 237n.

4

1. Andrée Hayum, "Meaning and Function of the Isenheim Altarpiece: The Hospital Context," in *Grünewald et Son Oeuvre*, p. 78.

2. An interesting and synchronistic problem developed in my efforts to translate the "le lendemain" passage from the Antonian reforms. When I originally saw that quotation, while doing research for my 1977 Jung Institute-Zürich thesis, I found it useful due to its mention of *feu infernal*, but did not have it thoroughly translated. It was quoted from Andrée Hayum's "Meaning and Function."

In Zürich in 1989, re-writing my thesis for this work, I was more serious about a translation, with but moderate success. I did, however, discover that the French "crotte" in the original meant "dirt, mud, mire, dung." The reform might then read: "The next day [the patient] must be brought to the ["crotte" = dung] entrance of the said hospital to be checked to know if the sickness is the infernal fire." The problem was that "crotte" did not fit well into the sentence. I was intrigued.

In completing this work in Pennsylvania, I came across Andrée Hayum's 1989 work *God's Medicine and the Painter's Vision*. Here, she presents a slightly different quotation from the Antonian reforms of 1478:

> Le lendemain le malade doit être admené a la crotte
> dudit hôpital (chapelle souterraine), et visité pour savoir
> si la maladie est du mal infernal; et s'il en est.

as opposed to her earlier

> Le lendemain doit être admené devant la crotte dudit
> hôpital et visité pour savoir si la maladie est du feu in-
> fernal. . . .

Her essay in the 1974 compendium gives the source of the quotation as "Chaumartin, Schmitt 341, p. 101." Her 1989 reference is confusing.

Dr. Hayum's translation of the 1989 quotation is "The next day they [the patients] must be led before the chapel of said hospital and they must be examined to find out if the disease is the infernal fire." Into the quotation comes "le malade" (the patient), not there before, and "(chapelle souter-raine)," also not previously included. No explanation is given for "la crotte," still intact in the second quotation. The only sense "la crotte" would make in the second version would be if the entrance to the subterranean chapel were muddy.

What happens in Dr. Hayum's second version is that dung is transformed into chapel. Instead of the patient's feces being examined to determine the presence of illness—a transla-tion that does not altogether fit the first reference either—the patient is taken into an underground chapel. Dr. Hayum goes on to say in her 1989 book that the Infernal Fire was discovered, in 1597, to be alimentary in origin, caused by ergot. Such a situation would make sense of an injunction, even in 1478, to examine a patient's stool, or "crotte."

A French-born friend of mine in Scranton, Simone Kiven, is of the opinion that "crotte" in the original is a misreading of "grotte," indeed an underground chapel. Whether a patient is directed to be brought before the altar for diagnosis, or whether the stool is inspected, the juxtaposition of dirt and chapel, evil and spirituality is joined even in the problem of translation. And even today. That is the issue in the Isenheim Crucifixion and precisely the point of my work.

3. Hayum, "Meaning and Function," p. 81.

4. Ibid., pp. 88–89.

5. Frank James Bové, *The Story of Ergot: For Physicians, Pharmacists, Nurses, Biochemists, Biologists and Others Interested in the Life Sciences* (Basel: S. Karger, 1970), p. 152.

6. Hayum, *God's Medicine and the Painter's Vision*, p. 28.

7. Bové, *The Story of Ergot*, pp. 153–54.

8. Ibid., p. 145.

9. Ibid., p. 160. And John G. Fuller, *The Day of St. Anthony's Fire* (New York: Macmillan, 1968).

10. Bové, *The Story of Ergot*, p. 142.

11. Ibid., p. 145.

12. Ibid., p. 144.

13. Ibid., p. 153.

14. Ibid., p. 287.

15. Ibid., p. 291.

16. J. L. Hendrickson, "Syphilis of Giroamo Fra Castoro with Some Observation of the Origin and History of the Word," *The Bulletin of the Institute of the History of Medicine* 2 (1934): 515.

17. K. A. Knappe, *Dürer* (no city or date).

18. Erwin Ackerknecht, *Short History of Medicine*, rev. ed. (New York: Ronald Press Co., 1968), p. 191.

19. See Hayum, *God's Medicine*, p. 20.

20. Citation cannot be recovered.

21. Thomas Parran, *Shadow on the Land: Syphilis* (New York: Reynal & Hitchcock, 1937), p. 38.

22. See Cecilia Mettler, *History of Medicine: A Correlative Text* (Philadelphia: Blakiston, 1947), p. 615.

23. According to my sources, *incortu* may be a medieval derivation of the Latin *incoetus*, to have sexual intercourse. This, however, does not fit with the final statement of the quote. For me, the meaning of *incortu* remains obscure.

24. Mettler, *History of Medicine*, p. 616.

25. See Parran, *Shadow on the Land*, p. 15.

26. Pierre Schmitt, *The Isenheim Altar* (Bern, Switzerland, n.d.), p. 3.

27. C. G. Jung, CW 9, ii, §270.

28. Quoted without citation by Susan Sontag in *AIDS and Its Metaphors* (New York: Farrar, Straus & Giroux, 1989), p. 13.

29. National Public Radio news program, "All Things Considered," 26 September 1991.

5

1. C. G. Jung and Aniela Jaffé, *Memories, Dreams, Reflections*, pp. 36 ff.

2. Edward Edinger, *Anatomy of the Psyche* (LaSalle, IL: Open Court, 1985), p. 149.

3. Primo Levi, *The Reawakening* (New York: Macmillan, Collier Books, 1987), pp. 2–3.

4. Ibid., p. 25.

5. *International Herald Tribune*, 20 March 1989.

6. C. G. Jung, CW 9, ii, §84.
7. I. M. Lewis, *Ecstatic Religion*, 2d ed. (London and New York: Routledge, 1989), p. 169.
8. Eugene Monick, *Phallos*, p. 69.
9. C. G. Jung, CW 9, ii, §§314 ff.
10. Ibid., §314.
11. Ibid., §315, n. 62.
12. Ibid., §316.
13. C. G. Jung, CW 12, §§23–25.

6

1. Mircea Eliade, *Images and Symbols*, trans. Philip Mairet (New York: Sheed & Ward, 1969), p. 9.
2. St. John of the Cross, "O Living Flame of Love," in *The Poems of St. John of the Cross*, trans. Willis Barnstone (New York: New Directions, 1972), p. 57.
3. Ibid.
4. Wallace Shawn and André Gregory, *My Dinner with André: A Screenplay* (New York: Grove Press, 1981), p. 111.
5. Erich Fromm quoted in Gerda Lerner, *The Creation of Patriarchy* (New York: Oxford University Press, 1986), p. 199.
6. Robert Sardello, "The Illusion of Infection," *Spring 1988*: 15.
7. Ibid., p. 19.
8. Ibid., p. 22.
9. Ibid.
10. *Roget's International Thesaurus*, 3d ed., entry 684:27.
11. Sardello, "The Illusion of Infection," p. 23.
12. Ibid., p. 22.

13. "Tantum Ergo," hymn by St. Thomas Aquinas, *The Hymnal* (New York: Church Pension Fund, 1940), no. 200.
14. John 21:20.
15. Thorkil Vanggaard, *Phallos: A Symbol and Its History in the Male World* (Independence, MO: International University Press, 1972), pp. 25, 32.
16. Eugene Monick, *Castration and Male Rage.*
17. See chapter 2 of this book.
18. John 2:1 f.
19. Mark 3:31 f.
20. C. G. Jung, CW 5, §522.
21. Hayum, *God's Medicine*, p. 89.
22. Luke 8:2 f.
23. Luke 8:3.
24. Anatole Broyard, *Intoxicated by My Illness* (New York: Clarkson Potter, 1992), p. xiii.
25. Rosemary Reuther, "The Sexuality of Jesus," *Christianity and Crisis*, 29 May 1978.
26. See James M. Robinson, ed., *The Nag Hammadi Library*, rev. ed. (San Francisco: Harper & Row, 1988), p. 145.
27. See Eugene Monick, *Castration and Male Rage*, pp. 20 ff.

7

1. *Grünewald: With an Essay by J.-K. Huysmans* (New York: E. P. Dutton; Oxford: Phaidon, 1976), pp. 5–6.
2. *American Collegiate Dictionary.*
3. Marie-Louise von Franz, in *Man and His Symbols*, conceived

and ed. C. G. Jung (Garden City, NY: Doubleday & Co., 1964), p. 202.

4. J.-K. Huysmans, *La Bas*, quoted in Hayum, *God's Medicine*, pp. 134–35.

Soul-Making Pathology

Dark Eros: The Imagination of Sadism
THOMAS MOORE
From thousands of pages of the Marquis de Sade's fiction, Moore crystallizes the "Sadeian imagination," revealing the hidden soul values in the shocking phenomena of sado-masochism. He connects Sade's themes of isolation, bondage, violence, black humor, and naive innocence with patterns in education, therapy, marriage, and religion. (190 pp.)

Masochism: A Jungian View
LYN COWAN
How do masochism and martyrdom differ? What is the pleasure in shame, humiliation, and submission? After reviewing the clinical literature – Krafft-Ebing, Freud, Jung – the author shows how the symptoms of masochism acquire religious depth within the realm of Dionysus, Lord of Souls. (137 pp.)

God Is a Trauma: Vicarious Religion and Soul-Making
GREG MOGENSON
"Here is a book that does not fear to look the Devil in his face and to embrace what there it sees" (Marion Woodman). Greg Mogenson brings religion and psychology together by presenting a theology of soul, rather than of the spirit. Faithfulness to the soul shifts our focus from the overwhelming nature of whatever functions as "God" to the small scale of daily soul-making. (167 pp.)

Archetypal Medicine
ALFRED J. ZIEGLER
Packed with case examples and medical data, this book offers psychological readings of asthma, skin disease, heart attacks, anorexia, rheumatism, and chronic pain. Challenges the philosophical basis of traditional medicine, exposes its shadow, and charges that the excessive interest in health betrays humanity's deepest nature which is neither natural nor healthy but instead afflicted and chronically ill. (169 pp.)

SPRING PUBLICATIONS   P.O. BOX 222069   DALLAS, TX 75222